The Five Essential Leadership Questions

The Five Essential Leadership Questions

Living with Passion,
Leading through Trust

R. John Young

Keane Publishing
Charlotte, North Carolina

Published by Keane Publishing, Inc.
www.keanepublishing.com

This book has been registered with the Library of Congress.
Young, R. John
  The Five Essential Leadership Questions: Living with Passion,
    Leading through Trust

Library of Congress Control Number: 2007942863
ISBN 978-0-9800373-0-2

Dedication

To my five most influential teachers and mentors, each of whom, in his unique way, asked me the essential leadership questions:

- Robert Young—my father
- John McLaughlin—my uncle
- B. J. Jagger—my undergraduate professor
- A. H. Ismail—my doctoral professor
- Jack Botwinick—my post-doctoral professor

Contents

Prologue

A Foundation of Knowing

Whether you are a young and aspiring leader or someone upon whom leadership has been thrust, be aware—today's work world is fraught with a diminished trust in leaders, unrelenting stress, and, despite all the theorizing about visionary leadership, an unsophisticated appreciation for the healthy organization.

This book is about the very personal questions that you must ask yourself if you expect to be trusted by your followers and by those with whom you must collaborate. These questions are essential because they differentiate the espouser of platitudes about leadership from the person who can truly define the *soul* of his or her business, engender trust throughout, replace stress with hope, describe how his or her vision will be realized, leverage all the talent within, and confront the saboteurs. This person is clear about what is non-negotiable.

Ironically, my motivation for writing this book originates from the most frustrating question posed to those of us who work with human capital and refuse to be marginalized, namely, "How does what you do impact the bottom line?" Such a naive question is often posed by people who see financial profitability as the sole criterion for organizational performance or for whom dominance and control are their only strategies.

In contrast, I see profitability in a much larger sense—one that speaks to the adaptability and sustainability of an organization. The ability to adapt is essential to good health, both personally and organizationally. When we fail to adapt, we die. It is sobering to learn the statistics of how many companies will eventually get sick and die, despite having been idolized only a few years earlier. Similarly, it is painful to counsel failed executives who thought they had the perfect business and marketing strategies, only to lose the trust and commitment of their employees, managers, and shareholders. It is only then that they realize the critical role of human factors in business execution.

It is sad to observe their assumption that someone else was taking care of their leadership responsibilities.

Organizational health, like personal health, has risk factors with their associated precursors. Outstanding leaders understand this subtle causation. For example, customer loyalty will not survive without quality products or services. All the training for and preaching about quality are no substitute for the creativity and diversity of ideas that already exist within a workforce and are waiting to be unleashed. This will not materialize without an environment of adaptability and openness to change. However, accusing employees of being resistant to change, while at the same time you foster a culture that lacks physical and psychic safeness, good morale, and commitment to quality, is also misguided.

Healthy organizations are led by *trusted and effective* leaders. Clearly, it will require a new paradigm if human capital is to enjoy its rightful place in contributing to enduring profitability. The essential questions that I challenge you to ponder are predicated upon my **Paradigm for Profitability**© (Figure 1).

Instead of viewing *profitability* as the "bottom line," I position it as the "top line" and ask the question "What is the immediate precursor to profitability?" For the sake of argument, I view *productivity* as the precursor to *profitability*. You may be highly productive but not profitable. Symbolically, the **Paradigm** suggests the oneness of purpose that derives from collaboration— a hallmark of productivity.

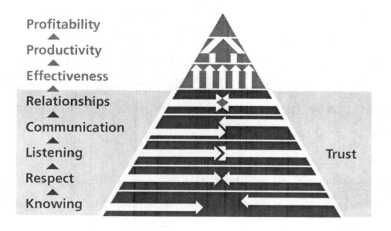

Figure 1

Profitability and *productivity* are different in the same way that education and teaching differ from one another. You may teach someone to be a pickpocket but you would not consider it education. Clearly, values enter the equation when educating. Similarly, teaching is a higher notion than training and training higher than instruction. At the other extreme, we encounter indoctrination. Leaders are educators who initiate followers into the discipline required for creativity and into the appreciation of the values that permit healthy organizations to endure.

Continuing down the **Paradigm for Profitability**©, the immediate precursor to *productivity* is individual *effectiveness*. You may train people to be effective, but there is no guarantee that they will collaborate with others. Instead, they may watch as their colleagues struggle to be productive, proclaiming that they did what they were supposed to do, but offer no more.

If these first three levels of the **Paradigm** are all we attempt—and in many instances this is what I observe within organizations—it is like flying an aircraft constantly on thrust, never benefiting from the aerodynamics of flight. We may never attain the altitude required to sustain *profitability* or create an enduring, trusting environment.

The world revolves on the quality of *relationships*. This is the case in international affairs, business success, education, and domestic harmony. In turn, healthy relationships require *communication*—the currency of leadership. *Communication* presumes that we *listen* to the other person. *Listening* presumes that we *respect* the person to whom we are listening. *Respect* presumes that we, in fact, *know* the other person, ourselves, and how others experience our character, personality, and behavior.

This sequence: *relationships—communication—listening—respect—knowing...is trust.* When relationships flounder and trust evaporates, we hear people say: "We didn't communicate," "He didn't listen to me," or "He didn't respect me." When we hear people say, "You don't even know me," we are in trouble. Therefore, knowing ourselves, how others know us, and being able to truly know others is the foundation of trusted and effective leadership. Wasn't 360-degree assessment technology created to sensitize the hard-driving executive to the importance of the foundational levels of the **Paradigm**?

When first presented with my **Paradigm for Profitability**©, people often remark that it reminds them of Maslow's[1] Hierarchy of Needs Theory. This is not surprising since Maslow, the pioneer of humanism in psychology, also illustrated his theory with a triangle-shaped model and argued for pre-conditional needs. At the base of Maslow's triangle were physiological needs; above them were safety and security needs; above them, the love and belonging needs; and, above them, the esteem needs. The pinnacle was the need for self-actualization. Similarly, I am arguing that we will never actualize true profitability if we do not attend to the foundational levels of the **Paradigm**.

Sophisticated leaders have deep insights into the power of the **Paradigm for Profitability**©. They understand what is meant by *profitability* at a particular time and place. They recognize that an error on any level of the **Paradigm** is enough to compromise trust and render the best of strategies impotent. Moreover, they see its application beyond leadership to business development and the appreciation of diversity.

For over 30 years, I have been coaching executives to lead healthy organizations by mastering the foundational levels of the **Paradigm for Profitability**©. Each level of the **Paradigm** has its own set of competencies that we measure, nurture, and develop within the constraints of the leader's unique character, personality, and behavioral style.

True growth begins with knowing oneself and how others experience us. While we can scientifically assess the quality of these relationships through our **Paradigm-based 360-Degree Assessment**, the most elegant and artistic skill of the educator, counselor, or chief executive is his or her ability to ask the essential leadership questions that permit the development of trusted and effective relationships.

How well do you know yourself? How well do you know the people you lead? Are you worthy of the trust of others? Can you cope with and lead change? Do you have the will to lead and truly understand what drives your desire? These are the essential leadership questions that must be asked and understood. These are the foundational questions whose answers will help separate and distinguish the authentic from the inauthentic, the grounded from the lost, and the true leader from the word itself.

In many respects, this book is a tribute to my father. He was a chef—and, as such, an artist and an actor. Every work night was a performance. But he never learned to drive a car. I was the first in the family to learn to drive and, fortuitously, was responsible, before I went to college, for collecting him each evening from his work. It was during our visits, as he unwound from the night's performance, that we talked about life. Among the many nuggets of wisdom he bestowed was the often overlooked truth that no one cares more about your life, your personal affairs, or your destiny than yourself.

Despite all the leadership development courses or mentors that may be made available to you, do not assume that another cares more about your development than you do. This book is your guide to self-discovery. Let's take this leadership journey together—and in earnest.

Part I

How Well Do You *Know Yourself?*

Chapter 1

Drawing from Your Life's Story

Life is just a chance to grow a soul.—*A. Powell Davies*

When did you realize you had leadership potential?

Your leadership development will start when you acknowledge that you have not tapped into all of your potential, have not integrated all of your talents, but, like a world-class athlete, are open to personal and professional growth.

The comparison to the Olympian is quite appropriate. Most Olympic contestants these days are physiologically and bio-mechanically comparable. Besides innate ability or talent, the winner is different either by biochemical cheating or by superior coaching—coaching that helps the athlete visualize the superior execution of his or her ideal performance.

I have watched many Olympic contests, both winter and summer. It is my tendency to listen past the promotional material to the athlete's life story. Two things are always clear. First, there was a lifetime of discipline behind the elegant performance. Second, the journey to greatness began very early in life.

Have you had the same preparation to be a leader? Do you want to enjoy the rich success of leadership or settle for mediocre power and a payoff that is cheaply gained? Remember, there is no luck except where there is discipline.

With every new leadership coaching assignment, the first thing I strive to discover is my client's life story. Where were they born and raised? Who raised them and initiated them into their culture of origin? What models did they have? Who sponsored or mentored them? What challenges were they faced with and how did they handle them? These conversations are the most interesting aspect of my work—getting to truly know the leader and his or her life's story.

Unlike the Olympian, aspiring corporate leaders too often define themselves solely by the academic degree they have earned or by the job title they currently hold—ignoring many of the life experiences upon which they can build a trusted and effective leadership presence and performance.

Your life's story contains powerful information about the influences that have guided, and will continue to guide, your life. The first step in knowing yourself is to examine the people, places, and things that are prominent in your memory and serve as significant influences and defining moments.

By way of illustration, I was born in the Glens of Antrim, an incredibly beautiful part of Northern Ireland, 16 miles by sea from the Mull of Kintyre in Scotland. Even though, as a family, we moved to London and most of my education, through my first degree, was in England, we always referred to the Glens as home and returned there at every opportunity.

From as early as I can remember, I returned home for the long summers to work alongside my Uncle John on his farm. He was my first professor—although, by his own admission, he met the students on their way home! They, like my mother, would have been on their way home from Glenaan School. It was a two-room schoolhouse next to the Old Mill, alongside the river Dall, where I spent my first three weeks of school.

As is the case throughout Ireland, every field and place has an Irish name. Tavnahoney, my uncle's farmland, extended up the mountain and was sheltered against the westerly wind and rain yet afforded the most beautiful views across the glen to Tieverah, the fairy hill, the town of Cushendall, the mountain Lurigethan, the peninsula Garron Point, and, on a clear day, Scotland.

I could literally go to town by gravity—after a few pumps of my bicycle's pedals. Days later the bike would be where I left it after I commissioned alternative transport back up the glen that night. It was a safe and magical place.

In the summertime, because of the northern latitude, the days were long and we spent most of our time in the fields making hay. Lunch and dinner were brought to the field. We drank either buttermilk, left over from churning butter on Tuesday mornings, or water directly from a natural mountain spring. When my uncle would stop to refill his pipe, I welcomed the respite from shaking and turning the hay. The pipe refilling was a laboriously artistic ritual as he would cut the tobacco from a plug, mix it with the remains of the last smoke, pack it down, and light the concoction with a Swan Vesta match.

At noon and at six each evening there was another respite as the church bells rang *The Angeles*. Everything in the glen stopped still. Hats were removed, and people either knelt or stood in quiet reflection, supporting themselves on their forks, rakes, or machines.

If we weren't saving the hay, we were on the mountaintop digging turf out of the peat bog and spreading it out to dry, later to be drawn by horse and cart down the mountain and stacked against the house for year-round fuel.

The long workdays were interspersed with community events such as sheep sales, cattle markets, wakes, funerals, and dances. Within the glen there were the nightly visits to neighbors. My uncle was a respected *Seanachi*, or storyteller. It was during these visits in front of the turf fire, and illuminated by a gas light, that I was first introduced to performing. In that society, we made our own entertainment. Everyone was expected to sing, dance, tell stories, or, as in J. M. Synge's masterpiece *The Playboy of the Western World*, tell tall tales. Performers were treasured. They were known, called upon, and honored with respectful listening.

In the Glens the poet was prince. By poet, I do not mean someone who purely rhymes words; rather I mean the person who can pack so much meaning, emotion, and influence into a few words and, with them, move others emotionally, attitudinally, and physically. Great leaders are poets. Not all poets necessarily aspire to be leaders, at least in the Western sense of the word.

I observed the potency of community each morning when my uncle would walk to the edge of the farmhouse street and study the glen. His eyes would search for every farmhouse and look for the smoke from the turf fire heating the water for the first cup of tea or boiling fresh found eggs. If there was no smoke, we headed to that house to ensure that all were safe. Similarly, when the hay was dry and ready to be built into ricks, people seemed to appear, without solicitation, to help their neighbor save that field. It was a community of interdependence. Everyone knew everyone else. Talent was everywhere. Togetherness was precious. It was safe.

Despite the beauty of the countryside and the pride of the people, there was always an undercurrent of sectarian strife beyond the Glens and within the province of Ulster. As I began my undergraduate studies at the University of London, it erupted into 30 years of deadly violence, fear, and distrust.

Today, Northern Ireland has finally some reason to hope for a peaceful future. Representatives of other strife-ridden parts of the world are even visiting the province to understand how peace was finally accomplished.

Regardless of what part of the world we live in, all of us have some paradigm from which we began our journey with both the good and the bad. Donella Meadows, the pioneering environmental scientist, reminds us that "Our paradigm is so intrinsic to our mental process that we are hardly aware of its existence, until we try to communicate with someone with a different paradigm."

I am convinced that my **Paradigm for Profitability**©, and its use in a variety of leadership development and organizational effectiveness settings, is a reflection of my subconscious observation of my own culture of origin. As in other tense parts of the world, Northern Ireland's environment epitomized fear and distrust, a lack of each community knowing the other, little respect for the others' views, a lack of listening, poor communication, and the absence of healthy relationships.

Lessons from the Warm Heart of Africa

I have heard many life stories in the course of my work. But perhaps the most poignant are those of numerous young leaders in Africa I have the pleasure of coaching and developing. These young men and women have stepped up to lead improvements in the health, education, and survival of thousands of orphans and vulnerable children within their local communities.

After suffering for years from the ravages of the AIDS epidemic, as well as famine and poverty, the people we would normally associate with leadership qualities, using Western criteria, are dead and gone. These young leaders, however, are taking the initiative to preserve their culture and its children, despite the fact that they have not had the mentors or models upon which to develop their own unique leadership presence. Working with them is so refreshing.

Using the same models and leadership curriculum I will share with you throughout this book, we are supporting the development of these evolving leaders; each of whom already has an incredibly powerful life story. Surely, through reverse learning, we will uncover qualities from which Western leaders might, in fact, learn.

Like mine, and those of the young leaders in Africa, some of your memories may be more intense or moving than others and, therefore, have more power to reinforce or transform your self-narrative. When reflecting on your life's story consider the meanings that are standard and the meanings that may be obscured, the truisms that are sustained, the voices in the margin that can be heard, and what resistances, if any, can be revealed.

Developing insight into the themes of your life's story permits more conscious choices and actions. For example, do you still hear the voice of your high school coach or teacher admonishing you about certain activities while praising you about others? Now consider the actions that may have been guided by the meanings and truisms specified by that voice, or accomplished in spite of them.

Understanding the Power of Myth

Sometimes we refer to these voices as the "myths" with which we were raised. "Myths" refers to central organizing principles, rather than to something that is fictional. One of my own myths was that failure was not an option. When we moved to London, the spoken and unspoken messages were clear. One message was that I had the reputation of the whole Irish race resting upon my shoulders and on my performance. Even years later, after I had graduated from the University of London, and my professor, Joe Jagger, sent me to study with Professor A. H. Ismail at Purdue University in Indiana—the same learned messages were equally poignant.

Our myths really confront us when we move from one culture to another. Such was the case for me moving from Northern Ireland to England, then to the corn fields of Indiana. At Purdue University, in the early 1970s, graduate students from around the world tended to meet at the International Center. It was there that I met my wife, Mary Pat, who was also its co-founder. The foreign students used to joke that we had to get traveler's checks to travel from West Lafayette to Indianapolis—only a 60 mile trip! Ironically, it was in graduate school at Purdue that I first experienced global diversity. As a leading engineering university, Purdue attracted graduate students from all over the world. The cultural diversity was both exotic and stimulating. We learned about each others' myths and developed a sense of safeness with, and appreciation for, diversity. The troubles in our respective cultures of origin seemed so far away.

Put the Oxygen Mask on Yourself First

These days, I consult all over the world, and I am always struck by the flight attendant's instruction to "Put the oxygen mask on you first before helping others." This is a great lesson for leaders. Self-assessment is essential if we are to truly know ourselves before even attempting to truly know others. Of course, "know thyself" was a principle invoked by Socrates more than 2,000 years ago and touted as a critical element of wisdom, peace of mind, and healthy interpersonal relationships. The great English poet Alexander Pope, in his *Essay on Man*, reminds us: "Know then thyself, presume not God to scan. The Proper study of Mankind is Man." Self-knowledge means that we have some level of awareness about how our attitudes and cognitions are related to how we behave, feel, think, and perform. It requires, for example, not just knowing that we do not like opening up in large groups, but understanding where this trepidation originated, or knowing the basis of this feeling, possibly a fear of coming across as anything less than perfect.

Cultivating self-knowledge is critical to becoming a trusted and effective leader. Firstly, through introspection and by comparing ourselves to others, we can get a clearer picture of the self that we would like to become—for example, the successful self, the thinner self, the more confident self, the winning athlete, etc. In other words, with greater self-knowledge, our hopes, fears, goals, aspirations, and motives become clear. Another consideration is that we can begin to see our self as more complex, that is, as occupying various roles (salesman, colleague, competitor) and having many characteristics (hardworking, persistent, responsive) that contribute to our ability to be resilient in stressful situations.

Self-knowledge can also increase our self-certainty or our self-confidence. Self-certainty is associated with both higher self-esteem and a greater sense of personal control. The Freudian ego-psychologist Erik Erikson[1] described self-certainty as "a persistent sameness within oneself and a persistent sharing of some kind of essential character with others—a feeling of being at home in one's body, a sense of knowing where one is going." By examining our feelings and rationale for an action, we can discover what responses are effective and generate new knowledge.

Knowing by Intuition

Reportedly, Albert Einstein had the following sign on his office door: "Not everything that can be counted counts; and not everything that counts can be counted."

How do you make decisions? Do you use subjective or objective truth; feeling or fact; intuition or rationality?

When deciding on hiring, firing, investing, or inherently understanding the *soul* of your business, it is often your intuition that is guiding you.

Self-knowledge is particularly advantageous as it is the cornerstone of intuition. We know by science, we know by faith, or we know by intuition. Intuition is difficult to define. I equate it to knowing but not necessarily knowing why we know. It has been described as the human form of animal instinct; knowledge based on experience or learned expertise that is instantly accessible. People with strong intuition seem to have immediate knowledge about a fact, or truth, as a whole and the awareness of past, present, or future events without the conscious use of such processes as linear reasoning, rationality, or analytics.

Rationality, in contrast, is a systematic way of thinking in which the thinker generates a number of linked propositions that can later be converted into assumptions and theories about truth. To polarize rationality and intuition would disallow the advantages that each approach to knowledge gathering and decision-making offers. Rather, it is the interplay between the intuitive and rational ways of acquiring knowledge that provides the greatest value and is viewed as a higher form of logic.

Intuition is thought to increase life satisfaction, yield better decision-making, and is also thought to lead to increased productivity through becoming more efficient and effective. To be sure, the twenty-first century world and economy demand inner qualities such as self-initiative, interpersonal empathy, and emotional intelligence. Intuition is required for all of these. Increasingly, intuition is being established as an important and effective form of information gathering in medicine, psychology, and business. So much so that many leading companies have recognized the value of intuition and offer "intuition training" to their executives.

Leaders of businesses know that there is not always enough time to research, produce reports, and analyze data in order to make important decisions. Often executives are faced with pressure situations in which they are required to make decisions on a crisis basis without sufficient time and resources. Successful executives clearly have an intuitive sense for the needs of the organization. They can see where it should be headed and know how to steer it safely into the uncharted future. Opening up to intuition allows us to be creative, experimental, and alert to opportunities and pre-emptive about exploiting them.

Marcia Emery[2], a corporate consultant and intuition trainer, is confident that you can strengthen your intuitive skills. Here are some of her tips for dialing up your natural intuitive ability.

- Get calm. If you cannot meditate, at least do some relaxation exercises or deep breathing. Take a long walk, work in the garden, or just retreat to a private room. Anything that quiets the mind will help.

- Look at a geometrical object or pattern (even if it is only in the wallpaper or wood grain) or listen to music that does not have words. These practices engage the right brain and help quiet the left brain.

- Play with intuition. Try to guess what someone will be wearing tomorrow, what a person you are meeting for the first time will look like, which is the quickest line at the bank, or which row has the best parking space.

- Keep a log of both intuitive hunches (also recording how you got them) and dreams so you can better understand the patterns of your type of intuition.

- Beware of emotional culprits such as wishful thinking and fear, which can sabotage your attempts. Stay as neutral as possible.

- Lighten up. Too much effort backfires, while laughter and fun help ideas and intuition flow more easily.

- Avoid rigid expectations about how intuition will come. Some people are visual, some notice different feelings in their bodies, and some may hear ideas.

Understanding Our Biases

While intuition, or using instincts and hunches, is a valuable and vital tool for leadership, recognizing that some of our instincts may be clouded by bias is equally important. We all have beliefs, values, a point of view, and opinions that shape how we receive information, how we make decisions, and what attributions we give to people and situations. Undeniably, it would be naive to presume that people are value-neutral or that they do not carry with them some form of bias. Invariably these biases have their origins within our life's story.

As the Talmud teaches us, "We do not see things as they are; we see things as we are." Do you know the biases you bring to your role as a leader?

Leaders who ignore their biases do a disservice to their employees and colleagues by unintentionally making assumptions based on personal judgments or experiences. There are several kinds of bias that can powerfully influence the attributions that both leaders and employees make within the workplace. Overall, the effects of these types of bias will shape the degree to which we reward or punish subordinates—or even our children.

For example, leaders who attribute poor employee performance to a lack of effort or commitment as opposed to ability or circumstances will take more corrective action and will also have negative or low expectations for future performance. Moreover, it is likely that future interactions with subordinates will be colored by these attributions. Over time, when people in leadership roles continue to respond to failure with punishment, the effect is often declining productivity, dissatisfaction, feelings of inequality, and negative affect among subordinates. We are more effective when we can realistically evaluate our personal inadequacies or limitations. This eliminates the need to cover up, blame others for failures, or pretend to be knowledgeable.

Counteracting Our Biases

The first step we can take toward avoiding the damaging effects that biases have on an organization is greater awareness of the tendency to see things from our own perspective. When we hold strong beliefs, it is natural to seek out information that corroborates these beliefs and to discount information that undermines them. By disallowing alternative information, we can grow blind to the actuality of a situation. Leaders must be attentive to how their personal biases slant their perceptions and keep them from knowing the truth.

Beyond self-awareness, there are other measures that leaders can take to ensure that they are operating with accurate information rather than previous assumptions or biases. For example, we can listen to employees' accounts or explanations for their behavior. Through active listening, we will make fewer internal attributions regarding employee behavior and engage in less punitive responses. Behavioral observation is a good way to decrease attribution bias. Researchers have discovered that leaders who routinely observe employee behavior are more aware of the external factors influencing performance and are less likely to make inaccurate attributions about them.

In order to avoid attribution biases, we should increase the interaction and communication among ourselves, employees, colleagues, and customers. People live in one another's shelter, as I learned in the Glens of Antrim. By reducing psychological distance, we will become more aware of the underlying causes for failure and be less likely to make inaccurate assumptions about others. In essence, this is working the **Paradigm for Profitability**©.

Children Go Behind the Moon

As a parent and an educator, and perhaps because of the influence of the United States space program of the 1960s and 70s upon my generation, it has been my observation that, metaphorically-speaking, children "go behind the moon" at about age 10 and, essentially, are out of radio touch! When they return, they leave home and may be gone forever. As parents, we may have less than 10 years during which to set the emotional and relational trajectory of our children or to share with them what we stand for and model ways to cope with adversity.

I was acutely aware of this phenomenon with my own children, Moira and Seán. In Moira's case, I resolved to take her on a month-long trip to continental Europe, a place I had never been before, having always come to America. When we exited Charles de Gaulle airport in Paris I said to her, "O.K., honey, (she was nine) get us downtown." "What do you mean?" her eyes and voice pleaded. "Moira," I said, "you told me you were learning French at school, I cannot speak a word of French. That is why I brought you!" She clasped her backpack and owned up, "But, Dad, all the French I know are the days of the week and the months of the year!" "More than I know," I said, and off we went. She rescued me at every turn. We have never forgotten that special time together. Today, we work together—and she still rescues me at every turn!

In the case of Seán, we started his pre-"behind the moon" trip in Amsterdam. On the train ride from Schiphol airport to the central train station I told him that we would carry our bags until our hands were sore and we could carry them no longer, then we would look for accommodations. We slept high above the central district and roamed through the heart of a uniquely diverse and tolerant city.

That particular year one of my clients was exhibiting at the Paris Air Show, which was our next stop. The highlight of our trip, however, was a visit with my undergraduate professor, Joe Jagger, at his retirement home in the southeast of England. It was such a pleasure to watch Seán and Joe, during that and subsequent visits, develop a special relationship. A generation is such a short period of time! It has been such a joy to share my teachers with my children. Sadly, such a natural process whether parenting, educating, or leading, has been lost in our fragmented societies.

I routinely tell these stories to the executives I coach. It really gets their attention. Periodically I receive e-mails from them proudly relating how they took a very special trip with their child before they "went behind the moon!"

Did you go behind the moon as a child? How did it impact your life's story? Did any of your children go behind the moon? Where would you take your children before they go behind the moon?

Questions for Reflection

1. What aspects of your life's story would others benefit from knowing?

2. What have you chosen or not chosen from your story to carry through your life?

3. If your life could be written in four chapters, what would be the title of each chapter?

4. Who were your heroes as a child and why?

5. Talk with relatives to obtain an understanding about your parents and their parents. Some useful questions are: What were the top three issues in the family? Who had the most power? What was the most important family tradition, and why?

Chapter 2

Standing for Something

It's not hard to make decisions when you know what your values are.—*Roy Disney*

Why do you think that others will follow you if they do not know what you stand for?

This is not to suggest that you should assert your religious or political views to others. Rather, it is to suggest that you should articulate the *soul* of your business and declare what, for you, is non-negotiable when it comes to your values and how you will live them strategically and through the execution of your business plan.

If you are embarking on your leadership career, it is imperative that you understand, from the outset, the importance of clarity around values, both to yourself and to others. Your values will set the trajectory for your career and give you the confidence and self-esteem to pursue your calling. Leadership is like a vocation. A vocation begins with values, commitment, and sacrifice. It also brings peace of mind and the satisfaction that comes from a meaningful, other-directed life.

Leaders Have Class!

Sociologists make the distinction between class and social strata. For example, you may enjoy the material benefits that derive from ascending through the economic or positional levels of social strata, but never be accepted by others as having "class." Class presumes an appreciation for, and commitment to, the essential values of the community. Trusted and effective leaders have class, a notion independent of cultural heritage, personal wealth, or present situation. Talking about *class* to the executive who is ambitious or driven is like talking about color to a person who is congenitally blind!

Do you have "class?" Or do others see you as a hustler? Who were your earliest influences? With whom do you associate?

I was initially trained as a teacher. To this day I can recall the first words from the professor who taught a class on the philosophy of education. On the first day of class he said, "If you do nothing else during the next four years, you must develop a philosophy of life." It was he who also taught us that we do not have to like the children we teach, but we do have to respect their right to an education. We do not have to like every employee, but we do have to respect their right to be safe, physically and emotionally.

I am always perplexed by the value we, in Western societies, place on different professions, at least as evidenced by how we financially requite them. Sadly, teachers do not fare too well. Biologists teach us that the most basic instinct in nature is the propagation of the species. Surely, the most basic instinct of a culture is its propagation. After the family, are educators not the most important? So what do we value? Do we dignify the profession?

While working recently in Malawi, Africa, on our local leadership development project, my colleague and I stopped to visit a primary school north of Kasungu. As our presence became known, children swarmed out of their schoolrooms and ran toward us with arms raised and waving—the traditional expression of excitement and greeting. One particular class caught my attention. The teacher was leading his pupils, most of whom were dusty and barefooted. He was proudly dressed in long pants and a long-sleeved white shirt with a tie.

While my colleague conversed with the group, I slipped away to view the classroom from which they had emerged. It had a dirt floor with single bricks for seats. I was moved by the joyful appreciation of the children and by the dignity the teacher retained despite the minimalist working conditions. He had class! In addition to teaching reading, writing, and arithmetic, he was also educating his pupils to have "class."

What are Your Core Values?

As the leader, you must be actively involved in generating and distributing your organization's core values. You cannot abdicate this responsibility to another or to a committee. In order for this to occur, you must determine your own core values and then practice these values. This is one of the most critical determinants of employee safeness, commitment, and morale. It is also the driver of trusted and effective leadership and the differentiator of the leader with "class."

Values form the culture of an organization and are reflected in its mission and vision. Values also influence the courses of action taken to achieve these ends, that is, your organization's strategy. Effectively, core values are a precondition for business excellence. As such, it is vital that core values are upheld by the entire organization so that employees are working together with a unity of purpose. By extension, belonging to the organization becomes the center of business excellence and gives the organization a sense of identity. There is no strength without unity.

Often, leaders assume that they can change culture by declaration. Initially, the leader, like the cultural anthropologist, must respectfully observe culture. They do not say to strangers, "I am here to change your culture." Many of the crises around the world today have resulted from such naiveté. We can, as leaders, however, impact culture when we are clear about what we stand for.

Because core values are intangible, it is tempting for leaders to focus on required competencies, goals, or results that can be readily identified. Unfortunately, core values are not the product of having the required competencies or even of having identified shared goals. Rather, core values reflect the leader's judgment as to what is meaningful or important in life and provide a yardstick against which personal, organizational, and societal behavior can be measured. It is not enough for leadership to control, arrange, and "do things right." Leadership must unleash energy, set the vision, and do the right thing. Consequently, it is essential for you to hold a profound understanding of the values for which you stand. Understanding your life's story as well as your vision for the future will enable you to clarify your values. When you are certain and have a strong conviction of the moral worthiness of your beliefs and business purpose, you will be able to build these values into your employees and your organization as a whole.

It is Easier to Succeed than to Fail

A few years ago I was staying at a Hampton Inn in Nashville, Tennessee. In the morning, when I came down to the lobby for the continental breakfast, there was only one seat available, across from an older gentleman. The humble and unpretentious gentleman indicated that the seat was untaken, so I joined him. I asked what had brought him to Nashville. He said he was there to give a speech at a local college, Lipscomb University. I asked the topic of his lecture and he said that he had written a book about which he planned to speak. I asked what the book was about, and he replied, "I am Truett Cathy; I founded Chick-fil-A. My book is entitled: *It's Easier to Succeed than to Fail*[1]." We chatted for a while and a few days later a copy of his book arrived at my office.

S. Truett Cathy is the perfect example of someone who knows what he stands for. Today, the Atlanta-based Chick-fil-A company is the second-largest quick-service chicken restaurant chain in the United States, based on annual sales. Currently, there are more than 1,250 restaurants in 37 states and Washington, D.C. Remarkably, Cathy has led Chick-fil-A on an unparalleled record of 38 consecutive years of annual sales increases. His approach is largely driven by personal satisfaction and a sense of obligation to the community and its young people.

His foundation, founded in 1984, grew out of his desire to "shape winners" by helping young people succeed in life through scholarships and other youth-support programs. The foundation annually awards 20 to 30 students wishing to attend Berry College in Rome, Georgia, with scholarships up to 32,000 dollars that are jointly funded by the college. In addition, through its Leadership Scholarship Program, the Chick-fil-A chain has given more than 20 million dollars in thousand-dollar scholarships to Chick-fil-A restaurant employees since 1973.

Truett Cathy is a devoutly religious man who built his life and business on hard work, humanity, and biblical principles. Based on these principles, all of Chick-fil-A's restaurants operate with a "closed-on-Sunday" policy—without exception. When not managing his company, Cathy donates his time to community efforts and teaches a Sunday school class to 13-year-old boys, as he has done for nearly 50 years.

In the words of Pubilius Syrus, "It is no profit to have learned well, if you neglect to do well." Truett Cathy's values are readily apparent in his restaurants. They are extremely popular and exceptionally clean, and their employees are polite and demonstrably vital. He struck me as a leader who was teacher and educator. There is no doubt that he and the people who work with him know the *soul* of Chick-fil-A.

I have observed that people like Truett Cathy, who stay vital well into their later years, share some common attributes. These attributes reflect many of the principles of Celtic spirituality so beautifully captured by John O'Donohue in his book: *Anam Cara*[2]—attributes that I was also taught to appreciate in the Glens of Antrim. For example:

- **Each day is a new beginning.** Mature leaders view each day as a new opportunity that is filled with hope and openings, not as a cage that will confine and stifle them. They look out over their metaphorical glen to see that all are well.

- **Notice everything around you.** Instead of rushing through the day, they take time to absorb the beauty of their environment, such as different colors, smells, and flavors. They notice also how their environment may be changing throughout the day, the week, and the months that pass. For me, shaking hay all day or driving sheep back up the mountain provided ample time to look around and observe the movements and listen to the noises in the glen. For example, a tractor struggling not to lose traction on a steep hill; half a mile away a bus letting people off, tracking their walk up the glen, and knowing who they are and what they are carrying by their speed and their gait.

- **See the world from different points of view.** Like the monks who lived in the classic round towers in Ireland, they move from one window to another and see the same world from different points of view. How are things different? How are things the same? The Irish race has been one of the most dispersed since the famine in the late 1840s. Moreover, the Irish people are among the most adventurous in the world. As a child, I always felt that people and news were returning home from far and wide. Today, that vital Diaspora is in real-time contact with the homeland via the Internet.

- **Appreciate the oneness of all things.** Instead of compartmentalizing, they believe all things are connected. That is, there is no rigid line between the physical and the spiritual, or between work and home life. Nor is there a separation between the generations.

- **The soul desires expression.** They know that within each of us is a desire to be creative, to be a part of bringing forth something new and unique. That is, to impart our essence. Note what people do when they are not at the workplace. Observe how they express their creativity in their after hours or weekend hobbies.

- **Each person has a particular gift to offer.** They know that each person's essence is distinct, which makes each gift a unique contribution. Each person is irreplaceable.

- **Work is where the soul of the person becomes visible.** They know that each person's "being" is expressed in his or her doing. Therefore, in many ways, work expresses who the person is.

- **Appreciate the soul of the business.** They ensure that the workplace provides a safe environment that satisfies the need to belong and do something extraordinary. Being able to describe that extraordinariness is to be able to describe the *soul* of the business.

- **Each person leaves an imprint through his or her work.** They create an environment for a person to unleash his or her creativity, his or her passion, and his or her potential. Like them, each person leaves an imprint through work, through his or her particular contributions.

Over the years I have worked with, or had line of sight to, many very successful leaders who made vital and constructive contributions well into their later years. To be sure, they took respites to rejuvenate themselves but were distinguished by the luxury of not separating work from play. In contrast, how sad to watch so many executives agonize about the labor of their work and count the days until their retirement.

Small is Beautiful

When I was a graduate student at Purdue University, I regularly attended an inter-faith lunchtime seminar, *Science, Theology and Human Values.* It was a fascinating mix of philosophers, scientists, and spiritual leaders. I have never forgotten our study of the 1973 book by E. F. Schumacher, *Small Is Beautiful*[3]. Schumacher was a respected economist who opposed the neo-classical economics by declaring that single-minded concentration on output and technology was dehumanizing, that one's workplace should be dignified and meaningful first, efficient second, and that nature is priceless. He proposed the idea of "smallness within bigness." For a large organization to work efficiently it must behave like a related group of small organizations.

Schumacher's work coincided with the emergence of ecological concerns and with the birth of environmentalism. He became a hero to many in the environmental movement. He argued for "appropriate technology," meaning that heroic technologies deployed in Third World countries would not create sustainable economies. Those of us who work globally can confirm that Schumacher's values and foresight are certainly being confirmed 30 years later.

Creating a Healthy Community

While it is fashionable these days to idealize the chief executives of large multi-national companies, I am more intrigued by the leaders of smaller companies that are often the backbone of a particular community. Invariably, these companies, and their leaders, eschew attention. The last thing they want is publicity. They know who they are, what they stand for, and are highly invested in their communities—economically, emotionally, and spiritually. Moreover, an employee's line of sight to the chief executive or owner of a small privately held company is much clearer than in a large public corporation.

Earlier in my career I was recruited by such a company. While still on the faculty at Washington University in St. Louis, I consulted to a small hybrid seed corn company, Edward J. Funk and Sons, headquartered in Kentland, a small town in northwest Indiana. It was owned by two young entrepreneurial brothers. Following the consulting assignment they asked me to join their company and lead the creation of both a healthy company and a healthy town. Initially, I was reluctant to leave the academic world I had been prepared for but saw the opportunity to create an even more intellectually appealing situation. I developed the company's human resources function from scratch, taught back at Purdue University, and founded a rural institute of preventive medicine that proceeded to apply to the National Institutes of Health for a grant to demonstrate how to create a healthy town and evaluate the methodologies employed.

What I designed was a neo-Framingham[4] type study (named after the ongoing longitudinal heart study in the Boston suburb of Framingham), meaning that I planned to track a whole community relative to improvements on certain health metrics while comparing it to a comparable (control) town 60 miles away. It was in the course of putting that project into action that I met the Indiana State Health Commissioner, Ronald G. Blankenbaker, M.D., who told me that what I was proposing was "prospective medicine." The application of the principles of prospective medicine began at Methodist Hospital in Indianapolis, Indiana.

Prospective medicine[5] is the science of estimating health risks and the art of communicating those risks to individuals and organizations to help them address current health concerns and make choices that improve their long-term health.

The investment by Bob and Don Funk was a reflection of their values and their commitment to the community where they were the largest employer. Unfortunately, that initiative coincided with the Soviet Union's invasion of Afghanistan, President Carter's boycott of the 1980 Olympic Games, and the United States' withholding of grain from the Soviet Union. That, in turn, resulted in the creation of a payment-in-kind program that compensated American farmers for *not* growing corn.

President Carter's decision changed the direction of my career. It liberated me to formulate my views on the nature of healthy organizations. In prospective medicine we evaluate an individual's genetics, lifestyle, environment, and access to care to estimate personal health risks. It was clear to me that we can do the same for organizations. (See Chapter 6)

What Do You Know?

Finally, when I am coaching an executive who is struggling with an ethical dilemma or with the choice between differing courses of action, I will persistently confront them with the question, "What do you know?" Invariably they know, deep in their hearts, what they should do. They know what actions match their values and the principles for which they stand. Sometimes listening to what you already know is difficult amidst the noise and stress in which you live. But you cannot claim deferred ethics!

Questions for Reflection

1. What is important to you today and has been important to you throughout your life?

2. If you could take only three things (not people) from your home, what would you select and why? How do they represent what you stand for?

3. Describe a time when you stood for something that others did not understand or value. How did their reaction or response impact you?

4. If what you truly stand for was engraved in granite and placed for others to view for centuries to come, what would be engraved? How would you feel about the lasting value of that?

5. Name three values that you have lived out with integrity during your life.

Chapter 3

Being Exceptional

When you saw me in the boxing ring fighting, it wasn't just so I could beat my opponent. My fighting had a purpose. I had to be successful in order to get people to listen to the things I had to say.—*Muhammad Ali*

You cannot build on quicksand. Yet many leaders either set themselves up to do so, or allow others to place them in positions that do not allow them to build upon the solid ground of that which they do exceptionally well.

A trade not properly learned is an enemy. God forbid that you would be under the scalpel of a poorly trained surgeon! What do you do exceptionally well? What is your sweet spot? As a teenager, I worked in a restaurant washing dishes and waiting tables. Like my father, I love to cook but, to this day, I wash my dishes as I go. It was a trade well learned.

Leaders who are clear about their own strengths are better able to capitalize on their assets. This kind of awareness can lead to both individual effectiveness and personal growth. Further, it is important for trusted and effective leaders to reflect on their own personal progress and improvement, and to celebrate it by conveying it to others and by rewarding themselves in some small way.

Discovering our strengths can be an enormously empowering experience. Empowerment is defined as the process through which our belief in our self-efficacy is enhanced, or belief in our powerlessness is diminished. Empowerment is important for successful leadership as it is a means through which we gain a sense of personal mastery. Empowerment can be accomplished through the provision of self-efficacy information and the removal of the sources of powerlessness.

What do your life's story and your values tell you about what you do exceptionally well? I distinctly remember where I was standing in the hallway of the psychology department at Washington University in St. Louis when Professor Jack Botwinick, who sponsored my post-doctoral research in the psychology of aging, asked where I had been raised. I told him Northern Ireland and London. He had just read the novel *Trinity* by Leon Uris. He remarked that he was unfamiliar with the history of Ireland: the famine, the struggle for independence, and the sectarian strife.

Out of the blue he said to me "You cannot wait for others to find out that you are good. Sometimes you will have to tell them." I later realized that he had observed in me the very Irish learned behaviors of working hard but not selling myself. Taking pride in our own accomplishments does not mean we are arrogant. Rather, it is a healthy way to foster self-esteem and confidence.

Some years later, I was working with the divisional leadership team of a major global telecommunications client. I had already worked all over the world with other divisions of this company. But I recall one particular day with this team of leaders at an off-site in Park City, Utah. I already knew each leader very well and, at the conclusion of each day, offered my observations about the human factors that could enable or compromise the execution of the business plan they had been discussing. As I heard about the marketing grandiosity, the millions of dollars involved, and reflected on what I knew about each person's personality and life's story, I realized that I was the only person in the room who had started a business from scratch and put everything on the line.

Character, Personality, and Behavior

Besides knowing our social history and its impact on our feelings, myths, and biases, it is vital to know how our character, personality, and behavior impact our effectiveness as well as how others experience us on the foundational levels of the **Paradigm for Profitability**©. Character, personality, and behavior are integral when evaluating the degree to which leaders are trusted.

Invariably, my new clients refer to all people issues as "personality." They confuse character, personality, and behavior and refer to them as one. Character is non-negotiable; personality is largely physiological and electro-chemical; behavior is the thing we are most likely to change.

Character refers to individual differences in our voluntary goals and values. They tend to be based on insights, intuitions, and concepts about oneself, other people, and other objects. Character indicates what we make of ourselves intentionally and is thought to begin developing at birth.

There are three dimensions of character: self-directedness, cooperativeness, and self-transcendence. Character assessment is a valuable tool given that low character scores, which reflect deficits in impulse control, empathy, and conscience, are associated with substance abuse and antisocial behavior. Conversely, an individual who is high on these three dimensions will display the ability to be effectual (for example, exercise self-control and work toward and achieve desirable goals); have integrity (for example, be truthful and sincere and follow through on promises and duties); and be committed to a greater good that transcends self instead of being self-absorbed (for example, is able to take into account the impact of one's actions on others in ways that demonstrate consideration for others)[1].

Abraham Lincoln reportedly said, "If you want to test a man's character, give him power." The most poignant characterization of character, however, that I ever heard was from my doctoral professor at Purdue University. Professor A. H. Ismail was born in Alexandria, Egypt. He represented Egypt in basketball at both the 1948 London and 1952 Helsinki Olympic Games. My four years with him were exquisite. He was a classical educator. We spent hours together talking about our research.

As part of the scientific training of his students, he had us present our research findings at professional conferences. Dr. Ismail was extremely demanding, exacting, and academically critical. In many respects his training included being humble enough to appreciate the bias we may introduce into the scientific method, be it in how we read the literature, design an experiment, conduct an experiment, analyze the data, interpret the data, or infer from the data.

He had three sayings that have stuck with me. Regarding whether someone knew themselves he would say, "You can't give what you haven't got!" Regarding peoples' competencies he would say, "That person doesn't know that he doesn't know!" His third was particularly chilling, "If you know the price of a man, kill him!" He told us it was a Bedouin expression.

Parents, professors, and executives effect character and competency development by inducing the right amount of frustration within their children, students, and associates. It is through the resolution of this frustration that character is formed and ethical behavior developed.

At the root of most human interactions is the assumption that it is possible to infer the mental processes of other people. This assumption is evident in countless domains of contact. For example, the testimony of witnesses in criminal trials, the use of proxies in opinion surveys, the interaction of couples in marital relationships, and indeed in corporate dealings with associates, colleagues, and competitors.

The inherent belief is that others' behavior is analogous to our own, and thus we presume (erroneously) that the other has utilized similar mental processes to arrive at that behavior.

Further, individuals tend to weigh negative behavior more heavily in making character attributions. That is, a single negative behavior can neutralize or cancel out countless demonstrations of positive behavior. As a result, we may find ourselves making character assassinations based on one or two actions that do not accurately reflect the personality and character of our colleagues or associates.

Personality refers to regularities and consistencies across contexts, over time, and between behavioral domains in the behavior of individuals over the course of their lives. Is the person who is dominant on the job also dominant at home? Is the person who is assertive today also assertive tomorrow, next month, and next year? Is the person who appears to be conscientious on a personality test actually conscientious when given the opportunity to behave in a conscientious way? The way in which people learn from experience and then adapt their feelings, thoughts, and actions is what characterizes their personality. A personality trait is a distinguishing, relatively enduring way in which one individual differs from another.

Above, I suggested that personality is largely electro-chemical and that the main ingredient that we can change is behavior. Does this mean we are stuck with our personalities and the personalities of our colleagues? Research suggests that while personality becomes more stable with time, it is an ever-evolving aspect of self that retains the potential for change[2]. As we age, we are thought to "become more like ourselves." There are four primary processes of change, however, that facilitate adjustment of personality traits. These include: responding to contingencies; watching ourselves; watching others; and listening to others.

Responding to Contingencies (that is, environmental socialization and expectations)—for example, roles such as being a manager come with specific expectations and demands for appropriate behavior such as acting industrious, serious, stable, intelligent, fair-minded, tactful, and reasonable. Thus, a person who is impulsive by nature would be expected to set aside his or her preference to make snap decisions in order to be an effective manager. Over a long period of time, meeting these demands and absorbing the subsequent reinforcing responses would contribute to personality change.

Watching Ourselves (that is, reflecting on one's own actions or self-insight)—continuing with the above example, if an individual is newly appointed to the managerial role and subsequently begins behaving in a more detached manner or decreasing personal connection, they may see themselves as acting less friendly with subordinates, a change that they then interpret as lack of interpersonal connection and perceive themselves as having diminished desire for sociability[3]. Likewise, when we become more self-directed at work, we are apt to become more self-directed with personal relationships and leisure activities.

Watching Others (that is, observational learning)—within the workplace, this type of change is facilitated most readily through mentorship between a senior member and junior member of an organization in which the mentor demonstrates role-appropriate behaviors and how to behave effectively in the organizational setting. Outcome studies suggest that mentored individuals report higher levels of career success, greater satisfaction, better understanding of organizational norms and goals, and higher salaries than non-mentored individuals[4].

Listening to Others (that is, receiving feedback)—a significant source of information about ourselves and subsequently a potential source of change are the people with whom we interact and the feedback they provide us. It is thought that people develop meanings about themselves through feedback from others. Thus, when individuals receive new feedback concerning their personality through employers, colleagues, or personal relationships, they may be more likely to change.

Unfortunately, in terms of empirical evidence, feedback has proven to be the least effective mode of personality change. This is because individuals often minimize or deny feedback that does not fit with their already developed self-concept. The most effective means for change include environment or system-wide changes that individuals must adapt to (for example, adjusting compensation packages to include metrics that are quality-related to help managers focus on quality) and a mentoring relationship or face-to-face contact with the immediate supervisor.

Psychometric Assessment

The first step in becoming a trusted and effective leader is to truly know oneself. Besides understanding the impact of your life's story and the evolution of your value system, knowing your psychological makeup is imperative. As the Russian proverb reminds us, "There is no shame in not knowing; the shame is in not finding out."

I am often asked if I can psychometrically determine who will be a leader. While I can develop some insights in this regard, I can be more precise regarding who will *not* be a leader. If someone cannot sell a life jacket to a drowning person, it is unlikely that he or she will convince others to follow his or her vision. A few years ago I was asked to coach a senior executive in a major automobile company. This individual was clearly a candidate for the top job but there was something missing. His extreme introversion compromised his ability to create a sense of safeness in others.

Differences in personality and behavioral styles are often the most clear when they hit us close to home. When my son Seán was between his junior and senior years in high school, he reluctantly accompanied me on a business trip around the world. I say reluctantly because he did not jump at the opportunity. Seán has always been an avid soccer player and a fan of Arsenal, an English professional football club based in north London. When I invited him to join me on the trip he initially declined, protesting that he had summer soccer camp obligations. I waited a day then tried another angle. I asked him if he would like to join me on a visit to see his grandmother in London. "Which way?" he enquired!

We had a wonderful time. We visited Tokyo, Hong Kong, Singapore, Mumbai, Zurich, London, and Atlanta before returning home to Charlotte. For him, visiting with his grandmother in London was precious. She asked him which, of all the places he visited did he enjoy the most. He replied, "Mumbai." It was there that the family of my best friend, Jal Mistri, spoiled us for several days.

But the most "testy" moment of the trip was during our stay in Hong Kong. We were there two days after Hong Kong was handed back to the People's Republic of China by the United Kingdom. There was an air of uncertainty about what the Chinese might do to the colony. But regardless, the city was as vivacious and passionate as ever. In the early evening we ventured out from the Excelsior Hotel to find a restaurant for dinner. I thrive on spontaneously immersing myself amidst local people. I love diversity and am a natural people-watcher. Seán was much more cautious than I. Eventually we found a restaurant, but the menu was only in Chinese! Seán was not pleased with me.

Shortly after we returned and school resumed, Seán went on his senior year retreat. That evening we sat down to dinner and he inquired, "What are you on that Myers-Briggs test?" "I am an INFP" I said. "That's it!" he retorted. "I am an INFJ." "In Hong Kong," he continued like a detective solving a crime, "you just wanted to walk out of the hotel and accept whatever happened; I wanted to know where we were going!"

Johari Window

The Johari Window[5] is a useful model describing the process of human interaction. A four-paned "window" divides personal awareness into four types, as represented by its four quadrants: arena, blind spot, façade, and possibilities. The lines dividing the four panes are like window shades, which can move as an interaction progresses.

	What You Know	What You Don't Know
What Others Know	Arena	Blind Spot
What Others Don't Know	Façade	Possibilites

- The Arena represents things that others know about you and that you know about yourself.
- The Blind Spot represents things that others know about you but you do not.
- The Façade represents things that you know about yourself but believe others do not.
- The Possibilities represents things that neither you nor others know about you.

Clearly, the ideal is that we aspire to realize our "possibilities" and our full potential. As we age, however, the blind spot becomes larger, both bio-mechanically and attitudinally. Similarly, the façade becomes larger as we become more risk averse. The arena then becomes more occluded, like an artery closing down, so that we are unable to respond to opportunistic insults in our personal or professional life. This is all the more reason we need to know ourselves to the fullest extent possible, how others experience us, and know and capitalize on what we do exceptionally well.

This closing down of the arena quadrant became very clear to me some years ago when my colleague, Dr. Kevin Denny, and I found ourselves referring clients to one another. Typically, these clients were executives who had worked for a small bank for 30 years but found themselves displaced as that industry consolidated and mega-banks emerged. I was encountering these executives in a career context and recognized that failure to adapt was causing some of them to become medically compromised. Kevin was encountering other executives in his psychiatric practice. They needed help reinventing themselves professionally. Together we were able to provide these executives with the support they needed.

Finally, just as it is important to observe and honor our own successes, it is equally important to do so for employees, the team, and the organization as a whole. This requires knowing the people you lead. Paradoxically, however, knowing others requires knowing yourself and having a high self-esteem and confidence. We must have adequate ego strength in order to know others. A strong ego identity allows us to communicate clearly with others and to view differences as an opportunity for growth rather than as a threat. With adequate ego strength, leaders can look beyond themselves to the needs of their employees.

Questions for Reflection

1. In what areas do others recognize you as an authority and listen to what you have to say?

2. Name one thing you can do better than anyone you have met.

3. If you could add to your existing repertoire of talents, one that would make you truly exceptional, what would that be? Is that realistically something you can bring into your life?

4. What is something true of you that you view as "normal" but others mirror back to you as admirable and exceptional?

5. What are the responsibilities associated with giftedness and being exceptional?

Part II

How Well Do You *Know the People You Lead?*

Chapter 4

Making People Feel Safe

**Oh, the comfort, the inexpressible comfort of feeling safe
with a person! Having neither to weigh thoughts nor
measure words, but pouring them all out just as they are,
chaff and grain together. Certain that a faithful hand will
take them and sift them, keep what is worth keeping, and
with a breath of kindness, blow the rest away.**—*George Eliot*

When you accept money from a company, purportedly to be leader, you give up the right to be ignorant about the impact you have on people. How well do you know how they feel? How safe do your employees feel with you as their leader?

By this I do not mean touchy feely safeness. Rather, I mean the physical and psychic safeness people feel when they believe that their leader knows where the organization needs to go and knows how to get it there, at the same time respecting his or her followers' need to express their unique talents through their creativity and its expression in the work they do.

Within each of us is a desire to be creative, to be a part of bringing forth something new and unique. That is, to impart our essence. Each person's contribution to an enterprise is unique. As John O'Donohue, in his beautiful book *Anam Cara*[1] reminds us, work is where the *soul* of the person becomes visible; where each person's being is expressed in his or her doing. Therefore, in many respects, the workplace is a sacred place and an awesome responsibility for the leader.

Three Critical Mistakes that Leaders Make

Over the years I have observed three critical errors that managers and leaders commit when interacting with employees:

- First, they confuse intelligence and academic achievement. Just because someone did not obtain a university degree does not mean he or she is incapable of making astute observations that may profoundly impact the success of a business.
- Second, they fall into the trap of thinking that employees are not interested in quality. That is counter-intuitive. The brain strives for the pleasure that derives from executing work with quality, symmetry, and form.
- Third, they assume that people are not interested in being led. Workers are desperate for trusted and effective leadership. They can tell the difference, however, between the true leader and the person who is scared stiff in his or her own skin.

Assessing Employees' Sense of Safeness

Pain is referred. Where you feel pain may be some distance from its source. That is why an organizational health effort and, by extension, the ability to execute a business plan, must have the bandwidth that covers all of the human factors across a business.

One way to assess how safe your employees feel is to examine your workplace patterns. For example, specific signs and symptoms of insecurity and stress in the workplace include excessive absenteeism, apathy, lack of teamwork, and poor motivation. These elements create staffing difficulties, decreased customer satisfaction, and decreased productivity and profitability. Another valuable measure is your own commitment to involvement in the workplace. Besides leadership involvement, employee participation and work-group encouragement and support are significant contributors to a safe climate or culture. A safe culture can also be engendered by leaders who express consideration for subordinates, that is, viewing them as human beings with needs, giving accolades when deserved, and, most importantly, displaying respect. Again, this is working the **Paradigm for Profitability©**.

Leaders are Coaches

Humans intuitively sense when others "get them." If you don't "get" your followers, you will lose your credibility as a leader due to an inability to steer others in the right direction. This is because an effective leader functions as a coach, guiding individuals toward their fullest potential. Essentially, great leaders, like great coaches, know their followers better than the followers know themselves. What is required, then, is a sophisticated understanding of people and their needs. Further, successful leaders appreciate that individuals are motivated by different factors, and they individualize their approach to members of the organization and the team, which allows them to get the best that employees have to offer.

Ascertaining your employees' expectations and discovering what drives and inspires them allows you to lead in a way that instills in them confidence that you will deliver, which will lead to safeness.

Creating a Sense of Community

Like my uncle in the Glens of Antrim, trusted and effective leaders can dramatically impact the sense of unity felt by people within an organization. Organizational and team unity allows businesses to attack problems as a collaborative unit. A divided company results in estranged relationships, corporate backstabbing, poor group ethos, and an inability to effectively handle change. On the other hand, it is well documented that unity through demonstration of the elements highlighted within the **Paradigm for Profitability**©, such as respect, listening, communication, and relationships, boosts safeness, morale, and commitment, and enhances worker performance. Feeling safe will also lead to adaptability, the true measure of personal and organizational health.

Clearly, therefore, creating a sense of community is imperative in creating safeness. Cultural anthropology teaches us that every culture has its own set of values, norms, attitudes, and ways of seeing the world. Each has its traditions, beliefs, behaviors, stories, and myths. Organizations are no different—they too have cultural characteristics, including their traditions, stories, and heroic figures.

The need to belong is one of the most powerful human needs. This sense of belonging, of being attached, derives from people sharing a common set of cultural attributes. Culture, for the anthropologist or sociologist, has an explanatory power similar to that of gravity for the physicist. If there is not an official culture with values, attitudes, etc., which employees can identify with and buy into, then one will emerge to fill the void—for the good or ill of the corporation. Classic psychological experiments dating back to the 1930s[2] and the 1960-70s[3] have provided volumes of empirical evidence that support this concept of the need for affiliation. Relationships bind us, one to the other, to organizations, institutions, and, ultimately, to society itself. In turn, healthy relationships are predicated on knowing, respecting, listening to, and effectively communicating with others—working the **Paradigm**.

A great deal of the scope of physical safeness is legislated and policed by government departments such as the Occupational, Safety and Health Administration, but there are broader issues here too, such as feeling safe from workplace violence. Psychic safeness presumes not only the absence of psychological abuse, but also the presence of a climate of tolerance and permission to fail. Creativity cannot flourish in an environment where people are not permitted to fail—no one is going to stick out his or her neck if there is a fear that it might be cut off.

As I mentioned earlier, do not assume that employees do not want to be led. A human resource approach to management assumes that humans desire to participate fully, to realize their "higher needs" of autonomy and self-actualization, and to identify with the goals of the organization. They will do so if the leadership and structure of the organization will permit it. People want not only to belong, to be liked, and to be respected, but also to contribute effectively and creatively to the accomplishment of worthwhile objectives.

Working the Paradigm

As you reflect on the foundational levels of the **Paradigm for Profitability**©, imagine jumping into the deep end of a swimming pool. Instead of wallowing half way down, recall that it is more efficient to go all the way to the bottom and push off the floor. You will reach the surface faster; so it is with the **Paradigm**.

Knowing Others

Knowing someone else requires the development of both an intellectual and an emotional union with that person. A first step in this process is to assume the role of others, or to see the world from their unique perspective. One characteristic of successful leaders is their ability to intuit the personal, overt, or latent needs of their employees. By assuming the role of others leaders are able to appreciate the life of others and learn what is important to them, what their needs are, and recognize the differences that exist between themselves and others. In getting to know employees, we realize the worth and value that each individual brings to the organization.

Some executives seem scared to know their employees. Perhaps they feel that to know an employee is to risk violating the law by discriminating against that person. The truth is that it is hard to hurt someone whom we truly know. It is for this reason that hostage takers are talked with at length by expert negotiators and encouraged to get to know their hostage, hopefully reducing the likelihood of harm being rendered.

Not long ago a young man shot a judge and a police officer in an Atlanta courtroom. During his escape he took a young woman hostage in her apartment. Instinctually, she talked with the escapee and introduced him to the book *The Purpose Driven Life: What On Earth Am I Here For*[4] by Rick Warren which had recently impacted her own life. She read to him all night, got to know his life's story, did not judge him but instead listened empathetically. We learned later that he felt she was the first person who took the time to get to know him. In the morning, he surrendered peacefully to the authorities. She had worked the **Paradigm**.

Demonstrating Respect

Do you believe that people would feel safe with you if they felt you did not respect them? Clearly they would not. Erich Fromm, the internationally renowned social psychologist, psychoanalyst, and humanistic philosopher, noted that "Respect is not fear and awe; it is the ability to see a person as he is, to be aware of his unique individuality."

There are two distinct descriptions of respect. The first kind of respect is due to people of particular standing; it is often required or imposed through the exercise of power or authority. In this case, you may think people respect you when, in fact, they fear you. Companies that focus on hierarchies that position one person in authority over the other can potentially damage the ability to have true discourse among employees by inhibiting the flow of dialogue from those in subordinate positions. Further, if employees feel coerced into doing their jobs, they may end up resenting the company and their work. The result can be substandard performance for the entire organization.

The second kind of respect is based on regard and attention. This kind of respect begins when both parties believe that they have something to learn from the other. It requires both an awareness of one's own self-identity and an acceptance of other people's self-identities. Respect allows for consciousness raising, shared power, and inclusion. Note that respecting another individual does not necessitate liking or agreeing with them; rather, it involves engendering a feeling that people are important, and that their ideas, experiences, and involvement are valued. Time after time, research confirms that respect is vital for true dialogue.

Some years ago I was referred to the founder and chief executive of a nationwide chain of stores. The individual was very intelligent, commanding, and demanding. He would summon members of his executive staff to his office and from behind a large oval desk he would proceed to de-humanize them. He seemed to take particular delight in doing so in front of a stranger. In all my years of consulting with leaders, he was the epitome of a destroyer of trust and safeness, and a violator of the principles of the **Paradigm**. He was not interested in being helped. Not surprisingly, the company went from being a household name to becoming extinct. I am reminded of that unhealthy leader each time I see the shadow of his company's name on buildings from which his signage has been removed.

Not long ago I witnessed the opposite demonstration of respect and listening. I was invited to The Pentagon to present my models and philosophy of leadership development to a group of admirals. The "noise" we typically see in a business setting was markedly absent. Respect and listening were afforded superior officers presumably because of the discipline inherent in the military training.

Dialogue Begins with Listening

As we move up the **Paradigm for Profitability**©, effective dialogue begins with listening. Without respect, listening can be filtered through prejudices based on gender, race, sexual orientation, nationality, social status, religious preference, political preference, lifestyle, etc. It is through knowing and respect that these filters can be reduced, and one is truly able to listen.

Karl Menninger, a psychiatrist and member of the famous Menninger family of psychiatrists who founded the Menninger Foundation and the Menninger Clinic in Topeka, Kansas, described listening as a magnetic and strange thing, a creative force. The friends who listen to us are the ones we move toward. When we are listened to, it creates us, makes us unfold and expand.

When supervisors listen, the trust, motivation, and performance of subordinates are enhanced. Listening is an active process in which the listener enlists the skill of physical hearing as well as the skill of critically detecting nuances of language, including those of body and word. It requires paying attention as well as calling for contributions at meetings, conferences, etc. Through listening, others are given the space to articulate their ideas and concerns, which will allow their perspective to be understood. Listening conveys that one values the other's unique input and enables an individual to become a skillful conversationalist, to inquire about topics that are of importance to employees, and to convey a message of caring.

A listening style determines what information is received, how, where, when, and from whom. Investigators have identified four distinct listening styles: people-, action-, content-, and time-oriented. A people-oriented listening style is characterized by a concern for others' feelings and emotions; this type of listener attempts to find areas of common interest with others. Action-oriented listeners prefer to receive concise, error-free presentations; disorganized presentations tend to frustrate the action-oriented listener. Content-oriented listeners are able to carefully evaluate facts and details before forming judgments and opinions and prefer complex and challenging information. Finally, time-oriented listeners tend to let others know how much time they have to listen and often have brief or hurried interactions. No style is considered superior; what remains important for successful leadership, however, is to understand one's own listening preferences as well as the listening preferences of those within one's workforce.

As the Irish proverb says, "Listen to the sound of the river and you will get a trout."

Displaying Cultural Awareness

Understanding listening preferences requires the listener to display cultural awareness, be sensitive to environmental cues, demonstrate behavioral flexibility, and rely on social composure. This is because there are cultural and ethnic differences in communication styles that play a large role in how effective one is at both listening and communicating. Given that today's workplace can be characterized as a multicultural, multiracial, and multilingual society, having cultural competence is an important ingredient for listening. To aid in cultural competence, distinctions in styles have been made based on culture; these are generalizations, however, and not true for all peoples of a given culture.

Individuals from Western cultures tend to exhibit "low context" listening. That is, they expect people to get to the point, assume that they do not have to rely on their surroundings for interpretation, believe that privacy is important, and take for granted that what is found in the verbal message is what is being communicated. For Westerners, the message itself is sufficient.

Those from Hispanic/Latino, Asian, Middle Eastern, or African cultures on the other hand, may speak indirectly, be more circular, focus on the context, use indirect logic and indirect verbal negotiation, and focus on nonverbal nuances. For individuals from these cultures, the message itself is not sufficient; rather, these listeners rely on context (including previous decisions and the history of the people involved) in order to obtain meaning from messages. Knowing what to listen for and how to listen facilitates effective communication within the organization.

Developing Effective Communication

Communication is the currency of leadership. It feels like a contradiction to suggest someone is a leader, yet he or she cannot inspire through communication.

Developing effective communication requires movement through the first three levels of the **Paradigm for Profitability**©. One must have knowledge of self and others in order to avoid ethnocentrism, show respect for others' differing views and behaviors, and listen before attempting to drive an agenda. Listening is required for effective communication.

Communication is defined as the human act of transferring a message to others and making it understood in a meaningful way. This definition focuses on the efficacy of communication in producing the desired effect rather than on the frequency or modality of information exchange. Indeed, communication is the quintessence of coordinating behavior in any organizational setting and is said to be the glue that holds together inter-organizational channels of operation.

As mentioned above, communication is an integral component for building trust and safeness among associates. The quality and sharing of information influence the success of relationships and are central parts of the relationship atmosphere. In companies with organizational hierarchies, power and status can negatively impact the quality of communication due to the inherent tension in superior-subordinate relations. Often, candor, openness, and authenticity are compromised when communicating upward (due to subordinates being guarded and defensive) and when communicating downward (due to supervisors coming from a command and control posture).

Effective communication draws on four dimensions:

- First, "professional style," or being articulate, clear, and well-spoken.
- Second, "personable," or being approachable and easy to talk to.
- Third, "direct and straightforward" communication is appreciated by both employees and customers.
- Fourth, being "sensitive to the needs of others," through listening and understanding the other's situation, is critical for effective communication.

Knowing the preferred method of communication, especially when crossing organizational and cultural boundaries, is imperative to communication competence, which refers to the effectiveness and the appropriateness of communication. For example, in today's fast-paced and technologically advanced world, while e-communication has been found to be efficient and useful, face-to-face communication remains paramount to generating quality personal relationships. Regardless of the type of communication used, the effectiveness with which it is communicated is an important aspect of our ability to succeed on the job and is cited as the single most important factor in building strong relationships.

Building Strong Relationships

As evidenced by the number of corporate failures resulting from executive misconduct, the true cornerstones of success are ethical deportment, integrity, and building strong relationships with employees.

Thus far, the **Paradigm for Profitability**© has described the foundation necessary for producing the kinds of relationships with coworkers, employees, and customers that are built on trust.

In teams, the building and maintaining of relationships ensure that individuals develop enough harmony to be able to get their group work accomplished. Of additional significance, when considering relationship building, is that the greater the differences between the organizations and cultures involved, the greater the complexity in relationship-building processes and the more time needed. In other words, when dealing with complex organizations, more time should be spent on the preceding levels of the **Paradigm** (knowing, respect, listening, and communication) in order to make possible the development of the kinds of relationships that lead to effectiveness, productivity, and profitability. Quality relationships help people navigate the processes that lead to agreed-upon objectives in a way that encourages universal participation and productivity.

Regardless of the methods used, creating a sense of safety and security for employees is indispensable for successful leadership and will attract others to follow you.

Questions for Reflection

1. Select five people from your personal or work life, and list two things that each person has needed from you in that relationship. What have you been willing to give or not give, and why?

2. Do you seek permission to address areas known to be "sensitive" in another person's life? Is there a way to seek "permission" to address issues with subordinates? Does that give away your power as a leader?

3. When was the last time you walked into the office of someone who reports to you to simply listen to them? Were you relaxed in their office (on their turf)? If so, or if not, why, or why not?

4. List five things that would help you feel "safe" in a work setting. Do you bring those same attributes of safety to those you supervise or lead?

5. How do you respond to peoples' anger, fear, and/or sadness? Are you reactive to those feelings in others? Can you stay close to others when they have those emotions and not be afraid or feel threatened or insecure around them?

Chapter 5

Knowing What Attracts Others to Follow You

As soon as you trust yourself, you will know how to live.—
Johann Wolfgang von Goethe

Leaders are attractors. Do you know what it is that attracts others to follow you? Do you know how others experience you? How do you dress? What is your leadership presence? How do you sound when you talk? Can your boss let you "out of the house?"

I sometimes feel that most of my coaching efforts with leaders are largely around this very topic. Take away your positional authority and you may repel people. As a leader, you are like an actor on stage manipulating the emotions of your audience. Ideally, that manipulation is to heighten the sense of safeness followers feel regarding where you plan to take the organization and how. That safeness will, in part, derive from their knowing what you stand for.

Leaders are Actors

So far, I have formally acted three times in my life. The first time was when I was an angel in my elementary school nativity play.

All I had to do was hold my hands a certain way and stare at the manger. The second time was more challenging. I was Charles in *Blythe Spirit*[1], the mischievous play by Noel Coward. The third time was a few years ago. I was Father Brest in John B. Keane's *Moll*[2].

Blythe Spirit was staged in Kentland, Indiana, when I was working on creating a healthy community. The director capitalized on my English accent. Acting was a lot of fun, and it taught me the importance of the director's role. It also reminded me of the amount and diversity of talent that resides in a community, no matter how small.

The producer of *Moll* was determined that I play one of the three priests in this delightful play about the housekeeper taking over the running of a small Irish parish. By that time, I was traveling extensively, flying all over the country and abroad, and thought I could not make the time commitment. But I was curious to see if I could *take* direction. In the end, it taught me much more than that. It taught me the incredible discipline required to make the story I was telling believable. Your believability as a leader is being judged every time you open your mouth.

My dear late friend Charlie Harrold epitomized so many leadership traits. He was smart, humorous, and loyal. He was the product manager for the hybrid seed corn company that sponsored my healthy community project as well as the town's mayor. Charlie could scientifically and poetically describe the differentiating characteristics of corn! The company's sales force loved to have him present to their customers. One evening, they roasted him at the Colonial Inn in Kentland, Indiana. Twenty four people, including me, spent an hour before dinner telling humorous stories on him. When the group was finished, he raised his hand and declared, "My turn!" He then proceeded, in sequence, to top each of our stories. What humor; what a memory! Charlie was an attractor. He was a magnet in a room of people.

360-Degree Assessment

A friend's eye is a good mirror. One of the most effective tools for personal growth and development, as well as leadership development, is 360-degree feedback. It is an excellent complement to the traditional psychometric feedback I discussed in Chapter 3 that helps the leader know his or her personality and behavioral style. 360-feedback goes further to help leaders know how others experience them, especially on the foundational levels of the **Paradigm for Profitability**©. In truth, 360-feedback was created to help the executive appreciate the importance of the foundational levels of the **Paradigm**, especially among those leaders who thought it was solely about operational effectiveness.

McLaughlin Young's **Paradigm-based 360-Degree Assessment** instrument permits observers (such as bosses, peers, subordinates, customers, and even family members) to rate the executive on the various competencies we have identified within each level of the **Paradigm**. Collectively, these ratings yield a score as to how trusted and effective the executive is perceived to be. Additionally, our assessment center correlates the psychometric data with the 360-feedback scores to evaluate the challenge the executive will face should he attempt to improve his performance on a particular competency.

Remember, you cannot give what you don't have. For example, if someone who reports to you is expected to operate on the fly (a typical competency associated with sales and marketing) but, psychometrically, is anal, a perfectionist, rigid, and couldn't sell a life jacket to a drowning person, you are trying to milk the bull!

The specific competencies we measure relate to each level of the **Paradigm for Profitability**©. Such feedback, when combined with the insights from knowing your life's story, what you stand for, and what you do exceptionally well, can provide you with the self confidence to truly "be" in your personal and professional relationships—that is, you will have mastered the **Paradigm.**

When I first visit clients, I am always scanning their professional "home." What does their office reveal about them? How do they want to be known? Is it their diplomas? Is it what others have written about leading? Is it posters with inspirational clichés?

In truth, leaders are educators and teachers. Who were your most inspirational teachers? I suspect they pulled you in with their ability to create a sense of safeness, respected your uniqueness, and encouraged you to dream. You would probably not be reading this book were it not for a powerful teacher in your life.

I was honored recently when an executive with whom I was working asked, "Have you always been a teacher?" After decades, since first being trained as a teacher, I am delighted that my clients acknowledge my commitment to their growth and development.

One of your major responsibilities as a leader is to educate, teach, coach, and mentor your direct reports so that they effectively execute the business plan. You must also ensure orderly succession by identifying and bringing along the next generation of leaders. If necessary, you may have to breathe fresh ideas and passion into the organization through the skillful recruitment of new talent.

Questions for Reflection

1. Are others attracted to you because of your power, prestige, and success, or because there are admirable qualities in your deportment as a leader? Is there a difference between those? If so, what is that difference?
2. What three traits are intrinsic to you that you believe draw others to you?
3. Name four people whom you consider "attractive" in your culture. Which of them have values that you would want in your own life? Which of those individuals have traits you would never want to be known for, and why?
4. Who is a leader that you would follow, or would have followed? Was there a time that this person failed you? If so, what was it about him or her that inspired you to continue to follow this leader, if that was the case?
5. What is the greatest challenge for others relating to you?

Part III

What Entitles You to *Be a Trusted Leader?*

Chapter 6

Building Relationships Based on Trust

To be trusted is a greater compliment than to be loved.—
George MacDonald

Do you feel entitled to be a trusted leader? Have you mastered the **Paradigm for Profitability©?**

The **Paradigm** is about intimacy. Sometimes executives have difficulty thinking about intimacy in a business context. They would like to compartmentalize their lives. Sorry, but it does not work that way. Leaders are well-integrated people. They are consistent between and among the various domains of their life. Moreover, they are very comfortable with intimacy.

The foundational levels of the **Paradigm** are trust. Trust is about safeness. When we feel intimate with someone, whether a politician, leader, or lover, we feel safe. We feel that we will not be harmed. To be sure, it can be an extremely fragile condition. Intimacy is the ultimate relationship. It depends on exquisite communication; undistracted listening; honor and respect for the other person; and an all consuming desire to know the other person. True leaders, in my opinion, are capable of intimacy and own the foundational levels of the **Paradigm**. Moreover, they are artists at its execution.

Leaders are also salespeople. They are selling their vision for their company and the strategies that will ensure its realization. Our study of salespeople reveals that high performing salespeople feel entitled to the business they pursue and can ask for it. Selling is the only profession where you cannot blame another for your failure. It is highly dependent upon establishing trust with a prospect. It is for that reason that the **Paradigm for Profitability**© has such relevance, not only to leadership and diversity but also to the success of business development efforts.

Trust is like being healthy or well dressed in that you do not notice it until it is abnormal or absent. When it is right, it is inconspicuous. For example, you notice the dandy or the tramp, the obsessive runner or the self-destructive person. It is only when there is an error on the foundational levels of the **Paradigm** that the hand goes up alerting us about the absence of trust. This can take the form of a union telling a workforce that they can deliver the foundational levels of the **Paradigm** better than management can. Or it can take the form of employee disengagement. By the time the symptoms appear, the pathology may be well entrenched.

Creating a System to Develop Trust

When I founded McLaughlin Young over 20 years ago, I assumed that everyone would appreciate the scholarly approach I took to solving human factor problems, for I was an authority. I had a rude awakening. Prospects did not want to hear about the science behind my work; they simply wanted to be sure that I could solve their problems. So I checked myself into a sales-training course. To this day I can remember the instructor's challenge: "If you do not have a system to sell, you will become part of the customer's system not to buy."

Prospective Medicine Approach

My "system" or approach to organizational health is strongly influenced by the principles of prospective medicine[1]. Prospective medicine, as I mentioned earlier, is the science of estimating health risks and the art of communicating those risks to individuals and organizations to help them address current health concerns and make choices that improve their long-term health. Prospective medicine grew out of the longitudinal Framingham Heart Study, in a community outside Boston, Massachusetts. Its tools, health risk assessments, are key drivers today in the battle against rising health care costs associated with highly predictable, yet highly preventable medical conditions. It is a refreshing contrast to heroic medicine, and the actuarial predecessor to the knowledge being derived today from the Human Genome Project. It is also becoming more relevant as we discover the physiological aspects of emotional intelligence.

The technology of prospective medicine is not only relevant to improving personal health but it also applies to assessing the health of organizations and improving their long-term viability and profitability. Just as a surgeon would not operate without a proper examination, an accurate diagnosis of organizational risks must be made in order for appropriate and effective interventions to be prescribed and implemented. Here too, we need to abandon the heroic approaches to organizational health.

An organizational diagnosis includes understanding the genetics of the business—for example, governance, structure, and legacy issues, such as those associated with mergers or acquisitions. Culture includes such things as values systems, symbolic structures, and traditions. The organizational equivalent of lifestyle includes how people lead, collaborate, and follow. Interestingly, for all the talk these days about leadership, it is my observation that most chief executives would love to have their direct reports collaborate instead of feuding, undermining, or sabotaging each other. Figure 2 graphically illustrates a prospective medicine approach.

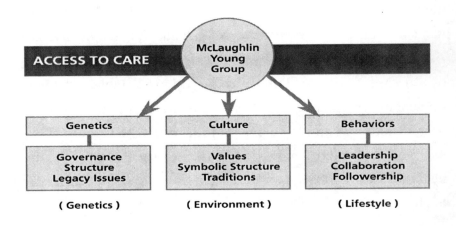

Figure 2

Any potential risks identified in the genetics, lifestyle, or environment of the organization are evaluated and addressed. This is vital since any gap in these areas will be sensed by employees and result in decreased morale and commitment.

Enhancing individuals' competence through development and ensuring that employees feel valued will also contribute to the feeling of safeness in the organization.

Too often businesses just do "stuff" without clarity as to why they are doing what, and in what sequence. Causation is critical. Similarly, a proper diagnosis of what impedes or sabotages trust within an organization is the logical starting point. To refer to the work on human factors as "soft" is naïve. It is extremely "hard."

A Prospective Approach to Organizational Health

What are the risk factors and the associated precursors to true profitability? Our **Six Circle Model**© (Figure 3) illustrates a prospective medicine approach to organizational health, the importance of human factors, and their impact on employee safeness.

Figure 3

"The worst crime against working people," asserted Samuel Gompers, the American labor union leader and a key figure in American labor history, "is a company which fails to operate at a profit." Healthy organizations seek to operate at a profit by achieving outstanding customer satisfaction and the equivalent of sales growth. This presumes that they have, and deliver, quality products and services. Many businesses use some form of total quality management to reduce defects and ensure quality. Too often, however, these costly initiatives fail because the human factors to support the processes are weak. I believe that quality is sustained when an organization embraces the diversity of its workforce and unleashes the creativity within. But that will not happen if the organization does not create an environment of adaptability and openness to change. In turn, that is unlikely to materialize if there is not a culture of employee safeness, good morale, and a commitment to quality. Ultimately, all of this depends on trusted and effective leadership.

Our clients usually come to us when they are in pain. We may initially engage with them in any one of the six circles (Figure 3). We strive, however, to rationalize the process of support. Knowing where we are in this model is what I call "organizational kinesthesis." Kinesthesis usually refers to the physiological phenomenon of knowing where we are even when we are disoriented. It relies on feedback to the brain from the balance centers in the inner ear and from receptors in our muscles that signal whether a muscle is tense or relaxed. The diver or gymnast who knows when to open from a tuck position just before he or she hits the water or the floor is a perfect example of "kinesthesis." Knowing where we are in organizational space and time is what

I mean by "organizational kinesthesis." Leaders absolutely own an understanding of this phenomenon, especially when they are confronted with highly complex situations such as large-scale organizational change.

As evidenced by the **Six Circle Model**©, we effect organizational change through the enhancement of each successive circle within the model. Each circle in the model represents a key condition necessary for comprehensive organizational health.

Trusted and Effective Leadership

The fish stinks from the head! When leadership is ineffective or unable to provide guidance, support, potency, and direction for subordinates, the entire organization suffers. Incompetent leadership is said to be the most stressful aspect of the job for workers; conversely, competent leadership enhances group performance and employee effectiveness and reduces absenteeism and turnover.

When a leader fails, it is most often *not* a lack of industry knowledge or expertise that leads to his or her demise; rather it is usually an incomplete knowing of oneself and others, a deficiency of respect and quality communication, and/or a paucity of meaningful relationships that erode the foundation for profitability and organizational health. As a leader, you must inherently understand the *soul* of your business, have a vision for the future of the business, and have the entitlement and followership necessary to be at the helm of reformation. More specifically, you must have the ability to make sound decisions in an environment of ambiguity and uncertainty; take the necessary business risks; avoid being insensitive and controlling; and be able to deal with difficult people issues. Added to this tall order is the fact that in the wake of accounting scandals, huge pay increases, and unpredictable stock markets, you will have to work even harder to gain the trust of your employees.

Employee Safeness, Morale, and Commitment

A corporate culture embodying safeness, good morale, and commitment is the backbone of a productive, innovative, and motivated organization—even in times of distress. In fact, after the terrorists' attacks on 9/11, it was observed that companies with a strong corporate culture were more likely to experience an *increase* in employee productivity. In contrast, those with unstable corporate cultures experienced upheaval, layoffs, and lost revenue.

Unfortunately, job satisfaction is on the decline. According to a recent Gallup poll, more than 70 percent of American employees are "disengaged," meaning that they have mentally checked out of their current jobs and are just waiting for the job market to heat up so that they can go to another one. The problem is often not that they are being overworked, but rather that they are not learning and growing in the work that they do. For this reason, people development is critical to keeping employees satisfied and motivated. An erroneous assumption is that individuals have fixed abilities and work should be assigned accordingly. This does not allow for them to stretch and grow. In giving the opportunity to grow and expand into tasks with greater responsibilities, individuals will be more invested in their work, and managers and supervisors will have fewer responsibilities to shoulder.

Adaptability and Openness to Change

Without the underlying ability to adapt and change, organizations will not remain competitive. Successful organizations may be tempted to hold on to processes that are working, following the thinking of "if it isn't broken, don't fix it." This is often because change can be difficult; but more and more organizations are recognizing that in today's marketplace, the main defense against obsolescence is not constancy, but rather flexibility and adaptability. That is, organizations must continue driving forward and reinventing their businesses even in times when the economy would suggest retrenchment.

Abandoning what has worked in the past is not easy. It requires understanding technology and the marketplace in order to know when creating new processes is going to enhance efficiency and productivity. It is important to combat the natural fear of change by identifying organizational risks and facilitating the creation of a culture of change. In identifying future risks or challenges, the human response to resist dramatic change is offset.

The **Three Circles Model©for Change** (see Chapter 8) illustrates ways in which many transformation efforts produce only temporary change. Based on scientific evidence, the model demonstrates that lasting change is the result of a clear overall mission or vision—what I call a "Third Circle." Indeed, as a leader you must have, and be able to articulate, a vision for the future of the company so that every employee knows and shares this vision. In order for this to occur, clear communication that flows both up and down the ranks is essential. This will allow associates at every level to understand the direction in which the organization is heading as well as what role they will play in its future.

Additionally, an accurate assessment of the strengths and weaknesses of those within the organization and of the organization itself provides a plan of action that will coordinate the critical balance across people, processes, and technology. Customized trainings (when combined with executive coaching and the resources of an employee assistance program) help individuals at every level in the organization to find this balance and ensure that all are working toward the greater vision. An essential piece of this is recognizing the unique contributions that each individual makes to the organization.

Diversity and Creativity

Today's employees encompass a wide range of cultural and ethnic backgrounds, speak different languages, practice diverse religions, may be from a single-parent household, or may have a same-sex partner.

Opportunely, a valuable factor for organizational effectiveness is heterogeneity. Heterogeneity is the extent to which diversity among group members involving issues such as personality, values, attitudes, abilities, skills, race, gender, decision-making, communication style, and beliefs is held as an important factor within the organizational makeup. This may at first be surprising, given the tendency to believe that the more alike we are, the more we will get along. On the contrary, groups composed of members having diverse, relevant abilities perform more effectively than groups composed of members having similar abilities. This is because heterogeneity promotes the opportunity for divergent opinions and attitudes, freedom of expression, and better decision-making by team members.

When operating smoothly, diverse teams and workgroups outperform homogenous groups on problem solving and completing complex tasks. Differences in understandings, values, and ways of viewing the world, however, can also create intra-team conflict. For this reason, diversity must be carefully and competently managed. Poorly managed diversity can lead to inconsistency, communication problems, and a lack of social integration. The result is low job satisfaction, higher levels of absenteeism and turnover, and ultimately low productivity.

Effectively managing diversity will enable organizations to be competitive in global markets that entail different ideologies, languages, institutions, customs, beliefs, social systems, and business practices. Moreover, leaders must be prepared to effectively manage diverse languages, cultures, ages, attitudes, and genders. This entails, among other things, a written policy for managing diversity as well as an atmosphere of respect and appreciation for the broader range of skills, talents, and contributions that diversity brings. Through assessments, trainings, and cultural integration, you can work toward correcting ineffective diversity management and support your clients by capitalizing on existing diversity within their organization.

Creativity is fundamental for organizational health. In fact, creating and learning are consistently acknowledged as two of the cornerstones of business excellence and productivity. Creativity can be promoted within work groups through autonomy in the work that individuals do, encouragement and support of creativity, a mutual openness to ideas while also constructively challenging new ideas, and shared goals and commitments. Healthy organizations accomplish this by focusing on five key factors: organizational climate; leadership style; organizational culture; resources and skills; and the structure and systems of an organization[2].

Quality Products and Services

A total quality initiative, such as the ubiquitous *Six Sigma* program, when supported by a focus on trusted and effective leadership, employee safeness, adaptability and openness to change, and diversity and creativity, can promote organizational health and ensure quality products and services. Given that the quality of products in general has improved significantly since the 1980s, a high quality product is no longer sufficient to claim a competitive advantage. Beyond the quality of the product, the consumer must feel a sense of personal attachment, or relationship, to the product.

Customer Satisfaction and Sales Growth

More and more organizations are recognizing that the company that cares about people, both the people who work there and the people who buy the products, will be successful in maintaining a loyal customer base. "Exceed the expectations of your employees," said Howard Schultz, the founder and chairman of Starbucks, "if you want to exceed the expectations of the customer."

Lessons from the Glen

I am often asked how my experiences in Northern Ireland and, in particular, in the Glens of Antrim have impacted my leadership presence and the corporate culture I have sought to create within my own company. At its core, the glen where I spent my formative years was not dissimilar to other rural communities I have visited elsewhere in the world. I recall the incredible pressure and expectation to please a guest or a visitor. That took the form of providing a feast, stopping everything we were doing to visit with the guest, or, upon their departure, walking them to the end of the lane.

A family's status in the glen was related to the quality of the work its members provided. Equally, there was no place to hide one's work or one's treatment of others. The disadvantaged or less capable were not marginalized; they belonged. Celebrations included all generations and drew out the talents of everyone. While tradition was treasured, adaptability was imperative. A person's character, personality, and behavior were on display for all to see. It didn't take a list of competencies for the community to know whom it trusted to speak on its behalf.

As a consequence of these experiences, it is unconscionable for our clients not to have their needs met, over and above their expectations. Our essence as an enterprise is manifested in the work we do. Respect for our employees is paramount. Their safeness, in all its manifestations, is a must. We are a creative community of scientists and artists; our clients are our guests; we trust and look out for each other.

If you do not have a system to create a trusted and effective community that liberates creativity and sustains quality, and makes a profit, you will become part of someone else's system. Often that someone is a saboteur with either a political agenda or a personal dysfunction that has no business being projected into the workplace.

Employee Assistance Program

That is why employee assistance programs (EAP) are vital to the health of an organization. An EAP helps workers and their household members manage issues that may adversely impact their work or their personal lives. EAP counselors typically provide assessment, support, and if needed, referrals to additional resources. The issues for which EAPs provide support vary, but examples include substance abuse; safe working environment; emotional distress; major life events, including births, accidents, and deaths; health care concerns; financial or legal concerns; family/personal relationship issues; work relationship issues, and concerns about aging parents.

An EAP's services are usually free to the employee or household member, having been pre-paid by the employer. In many cases, an employer contracts with a third-party company to manage its EAP. Confidentiality is maintained in accordance with privacy laws and professional ethical standards. Employers usually do not know who is using their EAP, unless there are extenuating circumstances and the proper release forms have been signed.

In some circumstances, an employee may be advised by management to seek EAP assistance because of job performance or behavioral problems. This practice raises concerns for some, who believe that the EAP may place the employer's interests above the health and well-being of the employee. However, when employee assistance is done properly, and with a highly qualified vendor, both the employer and the employee benefit. In fact, the goal of these supervisory referrals is to help employees retain their job and get assistance for any problems or issues that may be impacting their performance.

Pain in the body, and in an organization, is not always felt where it is originating. Our research on the impact of our employee assistance program teaches us that the festering finger will kill you! For instance, a festering finger causes pain and illness not only to the finger. If left undiagnosed and untreated, infection and illness will travel to other parts of the body. Festering fingers produce symptoms that are not limited to just the impact on the finger, or even the hand.

The same is true within organizations. Too often leaders underestimate the impact of human factors that are some distance from the leadership team but fester and eventually "take out" the leader and kill the organization. Festering finger symptoms are observed in the organization in the form of morale issues, absenteeism, talent retention problems, employee/leadership issues, and unmet profitability and productivity goals.

I am convinced that employee assistance programs are the most under-appreciated employee service. Employee assistance counselors deal daily with the symptoms of personal and organizational pain and observe the early warning signals of impending catastrophe. They are the first line of triage in a reactionary model of treating the festering finger! They see directly into the *soul* of a company and, at the same time, monitor the critical vital signs, and conduct preventative checkups.

Sadly, too many managers and leaders do not listen to these signals. In addition to all of the state-of-the-art services and global responsiveness available to our clients' employees, our clients' managers are trained to recognize and respond appropriately to the highly personal issues that can potentially derail a spectacular business plan.

One of the first services McLaughlin Young developed was an EAP. Our EAP deals with thousands of cases each year. I maintain that the two common denominators to all these cases are a sense of isolation and a feeling of hopelessness. When both of these occur at the same time, we have a potentially dangerous situation. Without an understanding of how this happens and a structure and language for leaders and practitioners to guide the organization, isolation and hopelessness at the individual level will grow into mistrust, employee dissatisfaction, cynicism, complacency, and decreased productivity.

Sometimes the mission of our EAP reminds me of my Uncle John's morning ritual of looking over the glen, checking for smoke rising from the chimneys of his neighbors' homes, ready to retrieve and care for those in need.

Promoting Trust

In order for you to promote trust, you must understand how trust is experienced and understood by those with whom you work, as well as the feelings, beliefs, and meanings that underlie trust. Most of the interactions that occur within an organization require trust. This is because most of the interactions also entail uncertainty.

Trust develops when successful behavioral interactions with someone are accompanied by positive moods and emotions. These affects create a feeling of trust and engender continuing positive exchanges and greater trust. When employees perceive the organization and its leaders to be competent, open, honest, concerned, and reliable while sharing values, goals, norms, and beliefs, the result is likely to be positive emotions and behavioral exchanges. These lead to favorable perceptions and judgments that the other party can be trusted and enhance the likelihood that the parties will develop shared interpretive schemes.

The distinctions in trust are not static. Rather they are dynamic and can shift from unconditional to conditional to even distrust when expectations are not met or negative mood and emotions dominate interactions. Therefore, it is essential that you continuously monitor the experience of trust within your organization. As will be seen, developing trust among colleagues and subordinates is a reciprocal process that moves through the **Paradigm for Profitability**©. Trust both requires and engenders knowing, respect, listening, communication, and relationships, and reciprocally, more trust. Trust is set in motion with the exchange of information and the development of positive attitudes toward each other, or knowledge of self and others.

Trust is the number one contributor to the maintenance of human relationships. Once trust is established, individuals are more likely to give others the benefit of the doubt. Without trust, however, individuals may not have faith, even when the truth is told. Studies have shown that work groups characterized by trust make significantly better decisions, are more open with their feelings, experience greater clarity about group goals, search for more alternative solutions, have greater levels of mutual influence, and express more unity as a management team. Clearly, trust is essential to your success as a leader and the success of your organization. Trust, however, is not easily manifested.

Remember that every interaction, communication, message, signal, or variance from the expectations of a relationship has the potential to diminish trust.

Questions for Reflection

1. Name three significant current relationships. What do those individuals do or say that communicates they trust you, or do not trust you?

2. Name a time you failed someone you respected or cared about. What specifically did you do to reconcile that relationship and/or situation?

3. Is it possible to be trusted in your work and be unworthy of trust in your personal life? What has happened in your life that informs you to choose that belief?

4. Among God, mankind, and yourself, whom do you trust the most and the least? Why? What has happened in your life to bring that about?

5. Identify whom you see as the most trustworthy person you have ever known. What qualities did this person have? How do you know he or she is trustworthy? What would have to happen for you to be more like that person?

Chapter 7

Sustaining Trust

You may be deceived if you trust too much, but you will live in torment if you don't trust enough.—*Frank Crane*

There is no need like the lack of a friend.

I frequently work with my daughter, Moira. If, in the course of our working with a leadership team, I do not mention the most difficult thing we as consultants deal with, she will take me aside and remind me to do so. She is referring to forgiveness. People have great difficulty forgiving, in both their personal and their professional lives. Many believe that they cannot put back together a crystal glass that has been broken. Yet forgiveness is one of the most interesting areas in health psychology, for the lack of forgiveness is very costly to our health.

Rich personal and professional relationships always have a subtle component of friendship. Friendship, unlike such institutions as marriage and parenthood, carries no legal bond or obligation. Friendships endure because of a delicate balance of acceptance and support. When one friend is more demanding than the other, and takes more emotionally from the relationship, the friendship will collapse. There is an axiom in the psychology of friendship that states: I cannot promise that I will not hurt you; but it will not have been on purpose.

Do you have a close friend? Do you have a friend who works with you?

True friends own an understanding of what it takes to sustain trust. Sometimes that may require making an apology. An appropriate apology, as my friend Dr. Matthew Alexander describes it, includes the supplicant taking ownership of the violation (I was a real jerk, I really wasn't listening); expressing understanding of the emotional impact of the offense on the other person (I know I embarrassed you); expressing deep regret in a way that shows some humbling (I am really, really sorry), where the tone of voice matches the words, an attempt to explain the reasons behind the behavior (I was jealous, I was distracted); and expressing intent not to have the offense recur (I will do everything possible to make sure this does not happen again).

Sadly, there are those occasions when a broken relationship cannot be restored as well as we would like. Distance, death of one party, or just the unwillingness or lack of ability may make reconciliation untenable or a bad idea. In these cases, breaches in a close relationship remain as trauma. These unresolved or unhealed traumas can be the most powerful in creating future bias or resistance to forgiveness and trust in people. It is these wounds that become the barriers to trusted and effective leadership and the saboteurs of working the **Paradigm for Profitability©**.

Fortunately, the science of human behavior has a relatively new field, critical incident recovery. We have also learned much from the field of human grief work. The knowledge from both these areas of human behavior has taught us that we are hard-wired, even after brokenness and trauma, to move on with our lives. We can even claim some wisdom and depth from the pain, which can often shape us into deeper, wiser people, and leaders. The work of Viktor Frankl[1], the Austrian-born neurologist and psychiatrist and Holocaust survivor, lends itself very well to addressing how we can rise, like a Phoenix, from the ashes of broken relationships. Elizabeth Kübler-Ross[2], the Swiss-born psychiatrist, has also become a resource for us in this area. The Recovery Movement also has a lot to teach us about making amends and moving forward.

The Challenge of Trust

No social institution, organization, or example of routine everyday interaction can survive without trust. It is the *sine qua non* of social life. Indeed, the social scientist Erik Erikson suggests that every stage of development that we negotiate through life begins with the challenge of trust (versus mistrust). In other words, trust is one of the very first lessons we learn as infants. The basic blocks of social life rest upon the establishment and the growth of trusting relationships.

When working with highly volatile workplace environments or while facilitating complicated change management initiatives, I resort to the lesson my wife, Mary Pat, modeled as we parented Moira and Seán. Regardless of the situation, she never spoke down to them.

She assumed a calm voice but, equally important, she physically placed herself at their level, speaking eye-to-eye with them. I find it painful to watch managers violate that simple lesson as they attempt to win the trust and confidence of their employees.

In the normal order of events, we live in a world of implicit, unexamined assumptions. We take so much of our daily lives for granted that we fail to notice what goes on around us. It has been suggested that the last thing a fish would ever notice is the water that it lives and swims in. In many ways, we are like fish and fail to recognize to what considerable extent even the most mundane aspects of everyday life are finely organized. During almost all our waking moments, we are bombarded with thousands of different stimuli—noises, smells, patterns of light, pressure on our skin, etc., but we seldom experience this relentless assault on our senses as an anarchic frenzy. Through the process of social perception, we make sense of our world by selecting, filtering, and classifying information. Thus, social perception is closely linked to the dual notions of making sense and forming impressions.

On the whole, we experience the world in a fairly stable and coherent fashion, precisely because of these unexamined factors. What all this means is that the world is basically explicable. We can explain a wide range of behaviors and place them in a context whereby they are *understandable*. It also means that social life is, in the vast majority of cases, organized and predictable.

Understanding Attribution

This brings us back to the role of trust in social relationships. Of central importance are the perception of trust and the attribution of trust in social interaction. Attribution is the process whereby we link behavior to "causes." In other words, how we *attribute* reasons, motives, and intentions to the actions of others provides us with explanations of why they are behaving the way they are. For example, if we witness someone behaving oddly (whatever that might mean in a specific context), then we will attempt to make that behavior explicable. We might classify the behavior as typical of a lunatic, or a drunk, or someone who is ill. At any rate, we attempt to explain the behavior by making reference to typical reasons, motives, or other frameworks of conduct or meaning.

Orderly and healthy relationships are dependent upon individuals attributing honest and above-board motives to each other's actions. The assumption must be that the motives and intentions of others are to be trusted. Imagine this extreme case: What if we assumed that every person we approached in the shopping mall or on the street was a potential mugger, murderer, or rapist; that behind every bush or wall there was a robber waiting to assail us? Social life as we know it would be impossible. This is clearly a situation in which there is *distrust.* Imagine this less extreme example: People are unsure of your intentions and motives. There is a high degree of ambiguity and uncertainty (which psychologically people find to be very unsettling). This describes an environment in which there is an absence of trust.

Without trust the possibility of organizational effectiveness, productivity, and profitability evaporates. Whether there is an organizational context of an *absence of trust* or one of *distrust,* the organization is in a bad state of health and is likely to be ineffective. The more morbid condition (that of the palpable presence of distrust) seriously undermines the organization and the sense of social cohesiveness will unravel. Under these conditions people will experience the world without perceptual coherence, and as a "noisy" and anarchic place.

The Power of the Paradigm

One of the best examples of the power of the **Paradigm for Profitability**© emerged during our work with a 200-employee, $100 million plant in a major city in the southern United States. The plant had been acquired several years before by a leading supermarket chain and was part of its extensive manufacturing division. The plant was in a rundown part of town and occupied a square city block. The workforce was almost equally African-American, Caucasian, and Hispanic. Following a bitter unionizing attempt, which the company narrowly won, McLaughlin Young was charged with understanding why the attempt had happened and with making sure it did not happen again.

Obviously there was a lot of anxiety among management when we arrived on the scene. Our solution was to apply McLaughlin Young's systematic approach to diagnosing the current situation, developing a shared vision of the ideal leadership and work environment, developing the plan, and providing the support to realize that vision. The intended outcome was to create a community of which all employees would be proud, keep the plant union-free, and improve customer satisfaction.

In the beginning, anger and hostility defined the climate. One of the first things we did was to enroll the plant's general manager in my seminar *Trusted and Effective Leadership—Reclaiming the Creativity to Lead Change.* This one was held at Ballynahinch Castle in the west of Ireland. There he met other executives dealing with similar challenges. Moreover, he developed a richer understanding of McLaughlin Young and our philosophy and approach. Trust developed between us, and he returned from the seminar serene, accessible, change-welcoming, and newly dedicated to involving others in the change process.

Following the principles of the **Paradigm for Profitability**©, we administered our *"Becoming a Trusted and Effective Leader..."* assessment protocol on the management team. It consisted of one-on-one interviews and psychometric testing designed to know the managers and in turn to help them truly know themselves and understand their hopes, fears, and opinions, as well as their strengths and weaknesses.

Typically, in these kinds of situations leadership tends to pathologize and blame the hourly employees. To counter this, and to reduce the debilitating stress within the plant, we customized our corporate health survey to prove that we knew, respected, and listened to the hourly employees. In addition to the survey, we held focus groups and interviewed every employee in the plant. We placed ourselves at eye-level with them. Taking the time to demonstrate respect and to actively listen to all concerned, resulted in a clear diagnosis of the current situation and a much healthier dialogue among all parties.

The employee corporate health survey showed that hourly people needed to believe that management knew them and understood their opinions, feelings, and issues of concern. This was demonstrated through meetings between management and hourly workers that were facilitated with precision by McLaughlin Young consultants. Some hourly employees, who were identified as "unreachable" in the group meetings, were brought into the fold through one-on-one work. As a result of the "knowing" activities, the climate predictably changed from being angry and hostile to being relaxed and open, a critical pre-stage to change.

The management team was then brought together in a two-day off-site retreat. The CEO's vision for the plant was confirmed by all—to remain union-free, to treat people respectfully, and to attain productivity and quality goals resulting in improved customer satisfaction. Aggregate results of all the "knowing" pieces were shared and discussed. A plan was created with six goals and their related strategies and tactics. Coping strategies for anticipated barriers to success were included in the plan.

The McLaughlin Young consultants spent intense time in the first two months leading up to and including the off-site retreat. Implementation and support of the plan were accomplished through monthly site visits and ongoing telephone and electronic communications. The project finished on time and all the goals were accomplished.

That plant went on to win the annual internal company-wide quality award four out of the next five years. Periodic employee satisfaction surveys revealed significant improvements in morale and a much calmer work environment. Employee stress ratings decreased. No one lost a job, the plant remained non-union, and customer satisfaction scores soared. I told the managers that they had completed an experiential MBA, because they had learned what it took to change the hearts and minds of their employees.

I also challenged the general manager to be extremely vigilant when hiring new staff, regardless of their level in the organization. First, discern whether the person is a giver or a taker. Second, does he or she respect the community the team created? And third, is the individual committed to personal and professional growth?

Remember, employees are forgiving, patient, relaxed and more engaged when their boss works the **Paradigm**.

Why Leaders Fail to Sustain Trust

Using the **Paradigm for Profitability**© we can see why some leaders fail to sustain trust:

- They fail to see the big picture and do not understand what truly causes *profitability*. They fail to see the crucial role that human factors play in the realization of profitability, focusing on the nuts and bolts (the *hardware* of productivity and profitability) while ignoring or downplaying human factors (the *software* that makes the hardware run).

- They cannot collaborate for *productivity*—an essential skill for executing the business plan. Modern organizations have to be organic in the sense that their survival and continual development demands relationships that are interdependent, collaborative, and characterized by trust. Paradoxically (given the importance of interdependence and collaboration), there has to be an organizational commitment to providing as much autonomy as it is possible to grant, limited only by the level at which employees are willing to accept it.

- They lack vitality and *effectiveness*, suffering instead from stress, anxiety, uncertainty, and guilt. These in turn are associated with a feeling of loss of control. Instead of the leaders taking charge of circumstances, circumstances are in control.

- They are destroyers of *relationships* instead of attracters of followers. They fail to nurture the human potential in their employees and corrosively undermine the avenue through which our social and psychological needs are met. There are basic human needs for affiliation.

- They cannot convincingly *communicate* their vision for the company. Either they simply cannot communicate or they lack the commitment necessary to realize the vision.

- They do not *listen* to their customers or associates, collaborators, or employees. Listening is never a passive exercise. Listening involves the active *attention* to what is being said. The listener must *attend* to the speaker. Paraphrasing Winston Churchill: It takes courage to stand up and speak, as well as to sit down and listen.

- They do not embrace diversity—the evidence of *respect*. Nor do they apply the golden rule, treating others as they would like to be treated—even for self-serving reasons. Leadership in this regard often comes down to the faithful exercise of human decency.

- They do not *know* themselves, their impact on others, or the people they lead. Without self-knowledge, how could it be hoped that they would know others or be able to empathize with them?

Lead by remembering what it was like to follow. This will inspire trust. Remember too that building trust takes more than twice the time it takes to destroy it.

Not surprisingly, each of these concerns corresponds directly with the factors highlighted in the **Paradigm for Profitability**©. This means that the leader who displays the competencies related to the foundational levels of the **Paradigm** will engender trust in his or her employees. Engendering trust is creating an environment that supports creativity and change; therefore, a leader must be a proponent of change.

Can Human Resources Sustain Trust?

In the Prologue to this book I noted that some leaders assume that others are taking care of the human factors in their business. Ideally, the role of the human resources function should be to act as a strategic partner with the chief executive. Much in the same way as the chief financial officer enables the financial capital, so should the chief human resources officer enable the human capital of the firm. There is still some distance to go before this is generally the case. Too many human resources professionals complain about being marginalized while doing nothing to empower themselves to be trusted and effective leaders and collaborators.

I have the pleasure of working with several human resources departments, however, which do enjoy that level of trust with their chief executive officer as well as help others to reach that quality of trusted relationship. They have managed to transform themselves from purely "transactional" to "strategic" human resources departments. They appreciate the importance of human capital and talent management.

As I reflect on my own firm's work during the past 20 years, it is interesting to recall how human factors have become increasingly significant in ensuring the execution of quality production. Imagine how that regression line will continue to track on an upward trajectory and necessitate increasingly sophisticated capabilities in the area of human factors.

Questions for Reflection

1. Describe a "falling out" with another individual where you shared some of the blame for the lack of trust. What did you do or say to retrieve the heart and/or trust of the other individual?

2. What five characteristics of long-term trusting relationships are essential to earning and sustaining trust?

3. How does forgiveness play a role in sustaining trust? Do you agree that practicing forgiveness has a role in the workplace? Why or why not?

4. Give an example of someone who is known to be trusted publicly, but that you personally would not trust.

5. In the midst of conflict with co-workers or subordinates what do you typically do or say to communicate that you value them and value resolution of the conflict?

Part IV

How Do You
Respond to Change?

Chapter 8

Coping with Stress and Change

It is not the strongest of the species that survives, nor the most intelligent, but the one most responsive to change.—
Charles Darwin

Leadership is almost never about maintaining the status quo; it is about creatively leading change. How well do you cope with the stress of change?

Often the terms "management" and "leadership" are used interchangeably. Management, however, is a process that keeps organizations running smoothly, keeps things in order, and deals with any problems that occur within the system. It is about managing transactions. In other words, management maintains the status quo (effectively and efficiently). Important as these qualities are to an organization's success, it does not fit within the definition of trusted and effective leadership. This is transforming leaders, teams, and organizations; it is promoting reasonable risk taking in order to harness innovation into a pathway for growth. As Neil Simon observed, "If no one ever took risks, Michelangelo would have painted the Sistine floor."

Successful and sustainable change initiatives are typically the result of superior leadership and a ready workforce combined with a sense of urgency. The leader has to be considered effective and trustworthy by the organization. Employees have to have the technical, systems, and behavioral capacity to engage in the change. Finally, the reason for change has to be so great that failure is not an option.

It is a challenge to find leaders who can effectively cope with the stress and drive change with an understanding of what their workforce needs to implement change. Moreover, change initiatives will be successful when the leader anchors the change movement in the very foundation of the organization.

Too often, leaders resort to blaming employees for being resistant to change. No one goes looking for a root canal! Invariably employees are acting in their own best interests and on what they know and feel. If the leader cannot clearly paint the picture of where he or she wants to go and how to get there, the follower is making a logical choice not to change. Until you have exhausted all of your ability to sell the proposed change, you should not *pathologize* your would-be followers for not getting on board.

This point is illustrated well by my experience with a food service client that was in the middle of a $40 million technology implementation to streamline financial and human resources systems. The leader (and the sponsor in this case) desired to "take a back seat" and "be there when it counts." She was able to articulate the business case to key executives, but the workforce and her human resources and finance departments were not clear about how the project was to be organized or how the project would be successful. Multiple projects with different sponsors competed for resources and attention from employees. Complicating matters for this executive was that she was new in the role. Filling the trust void were other formal and informal leaders. Instead of evaluating her own participation and effectiveness, the leader was determined to blame the employees for being resistant to change or "resenting her position." What would it look like if she had used the **Paradigm** as a foundation frame for managing the change for which she was responsible?

As I mentioned earlier in this book, in the development of organizational health I deal with three big issues. First is the pervasive distrust within businesses. Second is the impact of stress on personal health and performance. Third is the absence of what I call a "Third Circle."

Three Circles Model© for Change

Trusted and effective leaders define the future of an organization, align everyone with that vision, leverage the existing strengths, and inspire others to make the vision happen, despite obstacles.

After years of studying change theories and helping clients implement change strategies, I realized that I could significantly simplify how we talk about change. To me, change is as simple as one-two-three! I encounter my clients, whether individuals or organizations, in one of three circles. The "First Circle" is the current pain or desire. Emotionally, this is like being in the boxing ring with a kangaroo! I never know from where the left upper cut may come! They want to get me out of their lives, for I represent change. The "Second Circle" contains the wall that people and organizations hit as they try to get to their idealized "Third Circle." The "Third Circle" is the ideal state to which they aspire. But it is purely a dream without the process I am about to describe. In engineering terminology we help our clients create a "virtual design." That is, build their "Third Circle" before they build it. Or, as Wayne Gretzky admonished us, "Skate to where the puck is going, not to where it is."

The McLaughlin Young Institute has studied all of the psychosocial theories and practices relating to change and has incorporated them into our **Three Circles Model© for Change** (Figure 4). Because of its simplicity and animation, it has proven to be extremely powerful in helping leaders and followers see the need for change, acknowledge past failures, envision the ideal future, and make it happen. Our consultants and clinicians use adaptations of this model to help their clients understand their "First Circle," clearly see their "Third Circle," and proceed through the stages to realize their "Third Circle."

There are six stages through which a person or an organization moves on the way to the "Third Circle."

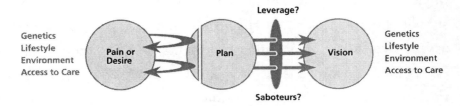

Figure 4

- *Stage One* is obtaining the correct diagnosis. It also consists of confronting the person or the organization with the realities of the situation. This stage is typically characterized by pain or desire, the two most basic human motivations. Here the leader blows the whistle on the unacceptability of the status quo. With his or her words the leader intensifies the pain the person or the organization is experiencing and gives life to the dreams and desires for the ideal. He or she can also describe the futility of past attempts to change: the denial, the learned helplessness, or the external locus of control. Remember that within organizations, as within the human body, pain is referred, meaning that it may be felt some distance from where it is originating. Heart attacks, for example, may be felt down the arm or up the neck. I am always amazed by how some chief executives will allow consultants to "cut" on their organizations without a proper diagnosis, something they would never allow their surgeon to do to them! In keeping with the prospective medicine model that guides our work we assess the genetics, lifestyle, and environmental factors that create the "First Circle" realities.

- *Stage Two* is seeing the ideal state, the "Third Circle," so clearly in one's mind's eye. This is probably the most crucial communication challenge for leaders. It is their job to poetically articulate the vision and mission for the enterprise and describe the *soul* of the business while creating a sense of safeness among their followers. In an organization, it is the leader who sells the pros of changing while creating a sense of safeness. Sigmund Freud once remarked "Everywhere I go I find a poet has been there before me."

- *Stage Three* is a clear description of what it will take to get to the "Third Circle." Need teaches a plan. Here the plan includes the strategies and tactics that, if properly executed, will provide the power to traverse the chasm between the second and third circles into which so many well-intentioned change efforts plunge.
- *Stage Four* is the leader tapping into the diversity and creativity of the individual or the organization and identifying the talents that already exist and are waiting to be unleashed and leveraged.
- *Stage Five* is an exposition, by the leader, of the potential saboteurs of the plan's implementation, a declaration of what is, to him or her, non-negotiable, and then acting on the obvious.
- *Stage Six* is the attainment of a new self or new organization with optimal vitality, quality, and profitability. Here, too, we see the new genetics, lifestyle, and environmental factors.

Yearly, we deal with hundreds of applications of the **Three Circles Model© for Change,** but one encounter, in a manufacturing facility in Detroit, brought home to me the potency of the model. This particular plant had experienced a union lockout eight years earlier and before my involvement with the facility. Employees hated coming to work and could not wait to leave after eight hours. There was an incredible amount of anger. Even younger employees who had been employed only a few months were protesting about the lockout years before their time. It was an organizational artifact that was embedded in the culture.

I systematically worked the **Paradigm for Profitability**© and got to know each employee, demonstrating respect and listening to the pain and desire of each person, their past failures, as well as their dreams. When I drew the **Three Circles Model**© **for Change** in group meetings, I could see the blood drain out of the employees' faces. I would graphically describe the attempt toward the "Third Circle," hitting the invisible wall; then circling back to the "First Circle."

Failure characterized everything they attempted. They saw their lives, both personal and professional, pass before them. They argued that all they needed was more money. I told them that I had no control over their compensation, but that I could impact their ability to see their "Third Circle," understand what it would take to achieve it, and do what it would take to realize their dream, whether within the plant or elsewhere. If they chose to stay; then at least it would be voluntary. If they chose to leave, they were in charge of their own destiny. That meeting, tense as it was, was the turning point in changing the hearts and minds of that workforce.

More recently, when I used a twig from a tree to draw the **Three Circles Model**© **for Change** in the African soil for the young leaders and volunteers we are developing, it was clear that they understood the realities represented by the model and embraced it with passion and hope.

Coping With Change

Companies that simply maintain the status quo will not remain in business. In the words of the American writer, publisher, artist, and philosopher Elbert Hubbard: "To avoid criticism do nothing, say nothing, be nothing." To be effective and generate safeness, you must lead, not just manage change. It is not surprising that research has revealed that coping well with change is one of the top three most commonly sought after characteristics of trusted and effective leadership. Coping with stress and change is a complex process involving our perceptions and emotions as well as the behaviors we utilize for adapting and changing.

Hans Selye[1], the Austrian-born physician and endocrinologist, was a pioneer in the study of stress. He developed his now-famous theory of the influence of stress on our ability to cope with and adapt to the pressures of injury and disease. He discovered that patients with a variety of ailments manifested many similar symptoms, which he ultimately attributed to their bodies' efforts to respond to the stresses of being ill. He spent a lifetime researching his "general adaptation syndrome." Selye served as a professor and director of the Institute of Experimental Medicine and Surgery at the University of Montreal. More than anyone else, Selye demonstrated the role of emotional responses in causing or combating much of the wear and tear experienced by human beings throughout their lives. He taught us that it is not the stress that kills us; it is our reaction to it.

Coping can be thought of in two ways: first as a "response" or a stress-specific pattern to prepare the individual, and second, as a "style" or a trait-like variable that is activated when the environment changes in some way. In this view, coping is similar to other personality qualities and describes tendencies to respond in specified modes.

In considering your response to change, it is useful to think of how the following three elements influence your response:

- the source of stress or the event, the stressor
- your cognitive appraisal or evaluation as to whether this event is irrelevant, threatening, or positive while also considering available coping mechanisms
- the outcomes

Appraisal and coping mechanisms mediate between the stress event and the outcomes, but it is the individual's personality or temperament that moderates the change process. In fact, it is thought that our static personality traits reveal themselves ardently under stress and impact appraisals and responses.

Believing We Can Cope

Someone with a high self-efficacy is more resourceful and less likely to allow stress to negatively impact his or her performance. That is, the clearer the picture of who one is and where one is going, the more stabilizing one will be in a changing environment. Other factors contributing to our ability to effectively cope with change include having a proactive mentality toward change and using it to our advantage. Further, tolerating paradox and avoiding being defensive when someone challenges cherished views will enable a leader to remain calm.

Leaders who display an inability to implement change, or fail to embrace change that is already outlined in a strategic document, often do this out of fear of the unknown or fear that the change will require them to alter the way they do business. This sends a poor message to subordinates and results in lost trust and credibility. Alternatively, to be effective, we must understand and utilize the change process. In truth, full commitment to personal views is not enough, because being a change *agent* requires attaining commitment from others, even those who do not agree with our views. There are no shortcuts. Instead, it involves the hard and potentially stressful, day-to-day work of culture shaping.

Act on the Obvious

Recently, I was supporting the human factor changes essential for a *Six Sigma* initiative to be fully deployed and optimized in a global electronics company. In the course of the work it became clear that there was not the level of discipline essential for the *Six Sigma* training to take hold. For example, meetings never started on time and ended only when someone else needed the room! Act on the obvious. Begin and end meetings on time. Failure to do so greatly undermines your credibility as the leader who can creatively lead change and cope with stress.

Questions for Reflection

1. What creates anger or anxiety for you in your personal and professional life? What premeditated steps do you use for resolving that anger or anxiety?

2. How would others say you cope with stress and change?

3. How many hours per week do you normally work? If in excess of 55 hours per week, do others inform you that your work hours are harmful to your relationships, health, or well-being?

4. Name three cases of unresolved pain from your past that you have struggled with in your adult life? What have you done to resolve those?

5. Does spirituality play a role in your ability to cope? Is there a place for spirituality in the workplace? Explain your answer.

Chapter 9

Developing a Healthy Mental Attitude toward Change

You must be the change you wish to see in the world.
—*Mahatma Gandhi*

We change either by shock, evolution, or anticipation. Shock comes with natural disasters or untimely loss. Evolution is a consequence of the aging process. Anticipation is taking a positive and proactive orientation toward our destiny, almost to the point of being change-welcoming.

In the organizational context, sometimes the challenges associated with a particular change seem so overwhelming, especially within large organizations or when dealing with international issues. But remember, the phenomena are the same; it is only a matter of scale and complexity. The principles of flight are the same for the large, long-haul Airbus A340, on which I fly to Africa, as they are for the little Cessna 172. Similarly, the saboteurs of the foundational levels of the **Paradigm** are the same in the Middle East as they were in Northern Ireland, and as they are in corporations and families.

You cannot remake the bed while you are still in it! Sometimes you will have to detach yourself from a situation and remake your world. I encourage my clients to start by taking a scientific approach to change. I remind them that the first step in science is observation. And, as with learning the performance attributes of any sport, the first challenge is to relax.

Recall Rudyard Kipling's 1895 poem[1], "If..."

> If you can keep your head when all about you
> Are losing theirs and blaming it on you,
> If you can trust yourself when all men doubt you
> But make allowance for their doubting too,
> If you can wait and not be tired by waiting,
> Or being lied about, don't deal in lies,
> Or being hated, don't give way to hating,
> And yet don't look too good, nor talk too wise:
>
> If you can dream--and not make dreams your master,
> If you can think--and not make thoughts your aim;
> If you can meet with Triumph and Disaster
> And treat those two impostors just the same;
> If you can bear to hear the truth you've spoken
> Twisted by knaves to make a trap for fools,
> Or watch the things you gave your life to, broken,
> And stoop and build 'em up with worn-out tools:

If you can make one heap of all your winnings
And risk it all on one turn of pitch-and-toss,
And lose, and start again at your beginnings
And never breathe a word about your loss;
If you can force your heart and nerve and sinew
To serve your turn long after they are gone,
And so hold on when there is nothing in you
Except the Will which says to them: "Hold on!"

If you can talk with crowds and keep your virtue,
Or walk with kings--nor lose the common touch,
If neither foes nor loving friends can hurt you;
If all men count with you, but none too much,
If you can fill the unforgiving minute
With sixty seconds' worth of distance run,
Yours is the Earth and everything that's in it,
And--which is more--you'll be a Man, my son!

Lessons from Elite Marathoners

Some years ago a leading exercise psychologist at the University of Wisconsin, Dr. William P. Morgan[2], studied the characteristics of elite and non-elite marathoners. He was curious about what psychologically differentiated world-class marathoners from weekend marathoners. Among his findings was that "the wall," typically encountered around mile 18 by non-elite runners, did not exist for the elite athlete.

He observed that the two groups were differentiated by their tendency to "associate," in the case of the elite, and to "disassociate," in the case of the non-elite runners. Elite runners were constantly in touch with their physiological, biomechanical, and psychological reactions. The non-elite tended to "disassociate," trying instead to distract themselves from the pain of "the wall." Do you associate or disassociate with the realities of the change process as you travel, step by step, mile by mile, to your "Third Circle?"

When I am consulting with a client who lacks a "Third Circle," I am reminded of another running metaphor. Recall how, as a child, we tended to run into the runner alongside us rather than stay focused on the finish line in the hundred-yard dash. Do you stay focused on your "Third Circle" and associate with all the stimuli that point to what you can leverage or what may sabotage your mission?

Positive Psychology

Positive psychology[3] is an emerging new field within the larger discipline of psychology. It has much to teach us regarding living with passion and leading through trust. It is the scientific study and pursuit of optimal human functioning that enables individuals, organizations, and communities to thrive. It focuses on human strengths and virtues. It builds on the science and research methods that helped us understand the "dark side" of human functioning, to help us understand how to capitalize on prevention and health promotion.

People want to be happy and lead meaningful and fulfilling lives, to cultivate what is best within them, and to enhance and integrate their experiences of love, work, and play.

This exciting new field has three central themes: positive emotions, positive individual traits, and positive institutions. Understanding positive emotions entails the study of contentment with the past, happiness in the present, and hope for the future. Understanding positive individual traits consists of the study of the strengths and virtues, such as the capacity for love and work, courage, compassion, resilience, creativity, curiosity, integrity, self-knowledge, moderation, self-control, and wisdom. Understanding positive institutions entails the study of the strengths that foster better communities, such as justice, responsibility, civility, parenting, nurturance, work ethic, leadership, teamwork, purpose, and tolerance.

We know that there is a set of human strengths that are the most likely buffers against mental illness: courage, optimism, interpersonal skill, work ethic, hope, honesty, and perseverance. Much of the task of positive psychology and prevention is to create a science of human strength whose mission will be to foster these virtues in young people rather that waiting for the heroic rescue so characteristic of Western healthcare.

Having a "Third Circle" is synonymous with positive psychology. How do you, your organization, or your community fare in the area of positive psychology? Are you practicing heroic management instead of trusted and effective leadership? Are you change-welcoming?

In the absence of a "positive psychology" approach to change, most people have a negative initial reaction. This is usually related to a perceived lack of *control* over their surroundings, their source of pride, or how they have grown accustomed to living and working. Safeness and security are perceived to be in jeopardy. This first response of shock is followed by some kind of reaction, followed by adaptation and change. Remember, the ability to adapt is essential to good health. When we fail to adapt, we die.

Some years ago, I was invited to make a presentation regarding the **Paradigm for Profitability**© to a group at the United Nations headquarters in Vienna, Austria. It was an impressive auditorium, and my remarks were simultaneously translated into numerous languages. The first comment from the audience, following my presentation, was, "But we are not in the business of making a profit." In response I asked, "Then why am I here?" Clearly the listener did not see beyond the financial criterion for profitability. The United Nations has a wonderful mandate, but it can be a depressing place. The lack of a "Third Circle" was palpable and the people I encountered exhibited the antithesis of a healthy mental attitude toward work.

Effects of Stress on Performance

Developing a healthy mental attitude toward change may be one of the most significant workplace challenges. Studies from behavioral medicine repeatedly reveal that prolonged exposure to certain job demands can lead to a variety of pathological outcomes. These outcomes can have both short- and long-term effects on emotional health (including emotional distress, depression, and anxiety); interpersonal relationships (marital difficulties and parent-child relationship issues); and physical health (stomach disorders, headaches, sleeplessness, cardiovascular disease, heart disease, and premature death).

In addition to the effect that it has on individual well-being, excessive work strain can impact participation and performance at work through decreased energy for work; burnout and job dissatisfaction; and even destructive social behaviors such as excessive alcohol consumption. Indeed, organizations as a whole are negatively impacted by occupational stress. This is because when employee well-being is low, organizations suffer financially due to increased absenteeism, lost productivity, sickness, and health care costs.

Locus of Control

A number of studies have focused on the attitudes of workers, their level of satisfaction and the meanings they attach to their work. Initially, these were linked to the level of automation and the degree to which workers could exert control. For example, lack of job satisfaction has been linked to assembly line production, and, more importantly, lack of control and autonomy. Conversely, high levels of worker satisfaction were related to greater degrees of control exercised by the employee and the possibility of making choices. It goes without saying that employees who are grossly dissatisfied and who derive no intrinsic rewards from their work tend to view work simply as a means to an end, and they are unlikely to make important contributions to corporate profitability.

When examining the issue of control, psychologists often speak in terms of an external or an internal locus of control. People with an external locus of control feel as though circumstances and events beyond their control impinge on them in such a way as to leave them feeling powerless. Things happen to them, rather than their making things happen. The individual experiences the world as external and coercive. The opposite is the case for those with an internal locus of control. They feel as though they do the controlling; they can make events and circumstances happen or at least manipulate them in such a way as to make the best of them. An internal locus of control is liberating and increases one's feeling of creativity, confidence, self-worth, and value.

Model of Occupational Stress

The "job demands—job control" model of occupational stress predicts that job strain, a stress outcome reflected in the physical and mental health problems noted above, occurs when jobs are concurrently high in demands and low in controllability[4]. Job demands can include working long hours, working at a fast pace, not having enough time, or having competing demands. These psychological demands lead to psychological outcomes such as stress and anxiety that produce the physiological response of arousal (elevated heart rate or adrenaline excretion). When control is low, the arousal cannot be appropriately channeled into a coping response, and the result is an even greater physiological reaction.

Conversely, when individuals have low control while occupying a low-demand job, the result over time can be learned helplessness, exhibited by an inability to make judgments, solve problems, and/or face challenges. Thus, the optimal arrangement for health, well-being, and productivity is to have a position that is high in psychological demands *and* high in controllability. In this instance, individuals tend to feel motivated, learn more, and have better health. In fact, studies dating back to the 1970s indicate that the mere belief in personal control, even when it is not exercised, has a significant impact on reducing stress and anxiety.

Indeed, extensive research indicates that the presence or absence of control within the workplace has tremendous effects on health and well-being, as well as on job performance[5]. Investigations have demonstrated that the degree to which employees have the potential to control their work is directly related to positive health- and work-related outcomes such as decreased anxiety and depression, decreased psychosomatic health complaints, increased life satisfaction, and increased job performance.

Throughout the day individuals interact with their work environment and some events are perceived by the individual as threatening or worrisome (perceived stressor). These can be work demands, conflicts among employees, or uncertainty about what to do or how to do it. The result of these stressors is an emotional reaction, typically anger or anxiety (negative emotion), which leads to strain (emotional and/or physical disturbance). Perceived control is important at each of these stages.

Individuals who perceive themselves as having control have lower negative emotional responses, exhibit less strain, and are less likely to interpret the environment as stressful[6]. That is, control allows the individual to minimize the damage that can occur in a situation, and accordingly he or she will have a less extreme emotional response. Control enables employees to perceive job stressors as challenges to be overcome rather than threats. Further, individuals who are free to decide how to accomplish a task or goal are intrinsically motivated and accept more personal responsibility for the consequences of their work, thus increasing job performance.

Perhaps even more costly to organizations than absenteeism, lost productivity, sickness, and escalating health care costs are the tremendous losses they suffer due to an inability to adapt and change. When an organization and its employees are under immense stress with little perceived control, their ability to adapt to changes in the marketplace, environment, and/or economy are significantly impeded. This is due to the tendency to have limited time and capacity for vision and to simply "react to the pain" without thoughtful consideration of appropriate actions. Thus, any changes fashioned when an organization or individual is under extreme stress and the perception of control is low typically result in temporary "band-aids." The outcome is increased strain on the organization as a whole and a decreased sense of urgency. For this reason, when contemplating the implementation of interventions designed to address current distress in the organization, the workplace environment must be considered.

For example, organizations spend an enormous amount of time fighting "forest fires" created by poor managers, lack of knowledge, absence of self-awareness, bad decisions, etc. These fires are catastrophic to a variety of stakeholders and burn uncontrollably. Fire prevention is significantly less expensive than the long-term cost of having to replace a forest. If organizations would just invest in fire prevention, they would not have to pay the penalty of being unprepared. However, too many organizations see training and development as a penalty rather than an investment in human capital. "It drains our funds," "It has no return," etc.

If the catastrophe and trauma created by organizational stress are not "prevented," or at least realized, it will have an even greater long-term impact on the organization—culture, employee satisfaction, recruiting, effectiveness. Sadly, most organizations allow the symptoms and behaviors resulting from stress to engulf them in organizational blazes that consume significantly more resources. Address the stress in a productive manner by trusted and effective leadership and you will prevent forest fires that will wreck your organization.

Individual Differences

To be sure, individuals require stimulation and arousal for action and productivity. Finding this balance can be tricky. While there are many benefits to increased perception of control for employee well-being, individual differences (that is, personalities), must be taken into account when determining how much autonomy and control each employee has within the workplace. Relevant personality characteristics include need for control, coping strategies, and self-determination. These traits will influence how much or how little control over his or her environment an individual requires.

For example, if an individual desires a great deal of structure, providing little or no boundaries around task allocation may lead to discomfort, anxiety, and strain. On the other hand, leaving little room for choice may stifle those needing flexibility and independence in the workplace. We have found that an experienced staff and battery of assessments help to flush out these individual personality differences so that applicable initiatives can be implemented. With appropriate levels of job stimulation and perceived control in place, the organization is then primed for interventions designed to increase leadership effectiveness, organizational performance, customer satisfaction, and sales growth.

The Case for Employee Involvement

Many companies, understandably, attempt to accelerate employees' adaptation to change. But those preoccupied with their internal processes are less likely to be fully productive. In fact, people in the early phases of change are often unable to do much at all, so it makes good business sense to help employees "cope." From the employee's perspective, such good intentions are often considered as controlling, even autocratic. If the change is hyped too much, some change recipients will start to feel isolated and resentful. How can you say everything is rosy when I feel miserable? A key factor in change initiatives not achieving their desired goals is the lack or mismanagement of employee involvement. Employees should be involved not only in implementing the change but in designing change plans and evaluating success. Information can be gained from the frontline that is invaluable in planning, implementing, and evaluating change.

In Chapter 7, I reported on a plant that won the quality award four out of five years following our organizational health intervention. As that success pattern emerged, I suggested to the general manager that we survey the workforce as to why the plant kept winning the award. Based on those findings, I advocated that he locate a local marketing firm to customize artwork and posters that related to their unique accomplishment—an accomplishment achieved through extensive employee involvement.

Interestingly, when the agency presented their creative ideas to a diverse group of managers and associates, their work product was perceived as simplistic and naïve. Half-way through their presentation an hourly worker interrupted the speaker saying, "You don't get it! You don't realize what we went through to change this place! This stuff is silly!" It was music to my ears. The employee involvement had paid off handsomely.

Healthy companies increase employees' sense of control and autonomy by involving them in the decision-making process. They are rewarded for their creativity and have information freely available to them. Indeed, employees have to be perceived as assets rather than as costs.

Change Does Not Happen in Isolation

When you are thinking about the impact of change, think also about the context you are operating in. Remember that few changes happen in isolation. The effects can be diminished or amplified by other things that are going on. Moreover, you have to deal not only with change, but also with peoples' reactions to it.

Even if change is adopted intellectually or it represents something positive, immediate acceptance is not usually forthcoming; instead time is needed to adapt.

Sir Edmund Hillary, who, in 1953, along with Tenzing Norgay, led the conquest of Mount Everest, notes that "It is not the mountain we conquer, but ourselves." Most people do eventually adapt to change but not before passing through some "psychological gates." The four stages that people typically move through are:

- **Shock**—from feeling threatened by the anticipated change, perhaps even denying its existence. We may "shut down" to protect ourselves, or deny the situation is occurring. Productivity is often low, and we feel unsafe, timid, and unable to take action, let alone risk making changes.
- **Defensive retreat**—we get angry and lash out at what has been done to us yet hold on to accustomed ways of doing things. We feel uncomfortable and unsafe and do not want to take the risks to change.
- **Resignation**—eventually we stop denying the need to change, acknowledge a loss, and mourn.
- **Moving ahead**—then we begin to think about taking risks and start exploring the pros and cons of the new situation. Each "risk" that succeeds builds confidence and faith, and we are ready for change. Change becomes internalized and we help others embrace change as well.

Charles Kettering, the inventor of the all-electric starting ignition and lighting system for automobiles, reminds us that "No one would have ever crossed the ocean if he could have gotten off the ship in a storm." Attitudes toward change result from a complex interplay of emotions and cognitive processes. Because of this complexity, everyone reacts to change differently. On the positive side, change is seen as akin to opportunity, rejuvenation, progress, innovation, and growth. But just as legitimately, change can also be seen as akin to instability, upheaval, unpredictability, threat, and disorientation. Whether employees respond to change with fear, anxiety, and demoralization as opposed to excitement and confidence (or somewhere in between) depends on the individual's psychological makeup, management's actions, and the specific nature of the change.

Typical Reactions to Change

It is important for you as a leader to recognize the typical reactions to change so that you can anticipate them and respond accordingly. By grasping more firmly the experience of being changed, you can gain a broader understanding of the effects, intended and unintended, of the changes you are instituting.

Any change, even a positive one, can provoke anxiety because it may be linked to loss of sense of self, status, identity, or meaning of work. With change, people often feel they are losing part of themselves. They may feel diminished in some way during the transition period, experience strong emotions, and feel unappreciated. Typical responses are:

- **Uninformed certainty**—we have confidence about the change in spite of a serious lack of data.
- **Informed doubt**—we become more pessimistic as we realize there will be significant challenges that we will have to overcome.

- **Realistic concern**—as we learn more about the downsides of the change, we develop plans to overcome the challenges. Confidence and comfort increase.
- **Informed certainty**—we are satisfied with the solutions we have developed and feel comfortable with the change.

Rethinking Resistance to Change

As I mentioned in the previous chapter, too often leaders resort to blaming employees for being resistant to change. Until you have exhausted all of your ability to sell a proposed change, you should not *pathologize* others. Resistance to change has become a catchall phrase describing the reactions of those who do not change as fast as we want or who seemingly will not budge. As such, "resistance" is considered an obstacle, something to be overcome during the change process. I believe we should view resistance as a normal part of adaptation, something most of us do, whether we know why or not. Instead, we need to take a scientific approach to understanding resistance and artistically facilitate our followers' movement through the stages of change. This requires anticipating, planning for, and investing the resources to address change. Remember, resistance denotes energy, energy that can be worked with and redirected.

We tend to label those who are resistant as having poor attitudes, lacking in team spirit, not being part of the forward movement. Yet, it is a normal response to think, "Why would I change; for what?" Resistant attitudes may reflect the frustration associated with learning new and difficult skills rather than nay-saying. In truth, the person may be genuinely trying to make the change, which should be encouraged. Use your listening skills. For example, the person's criticisms might provide clues that their training has lacked something. Rethink resistance so that you think of it as a natural process of self-protection, as a positive step toward change, as energy to work with, as information critical to the change process, and as an opportunity, not a roadblock.

To ensure a successful change it is necessary to use strategic thinking and all of our influencing skills to create a "Third Circle" and identify those crucial, early steps toward its realization. This will require accentuating the need to communicate industry trends, leadership ideas, best practices, and competitive analysis.

Competencies of Change Leaders

Successful change agents masterfully use their communication skills to build consensus for an organizational change. They are clear about their "Third Circle." They know that resistance is a consequence of the natural reaction to fear, namely, to be wary of change. Change leaders are people who know how to conceive and lead productive and effective projects, initiatives, or ventures that bring new ideas into use. They combine a mastery of the **Three Circles Model© for Change** and the **Paradigm for Profitability©**.

Despite the type of change, there is a generic set of skills found in the people who lead successful change efforts. They generate ideas, sell them, and implement them. Rosabeth Moss Kanter, who holds the Ernest L. Arbuckle Professorship at Harvard Business School and specializes in strategy, innovation, and leadership for change, has identified several competencies of change agents. For example, they:

- Sense new ideas emerging on the horizon.
- Sense problems and weaknesses before they represent full-blown threats.
- Identify gaps between what is and what could be.
- Become idea scouts, attentive to early signs of discontinuity, disruption, threat, or opportunity.
- Are never quite satisfied, even with success.
- Are very mindful.
- Possess kaleidoscope thinking: stimulating breakthrough ideas.
- Set the theme and communicate inspiring visions.
- Enlist backers and supporters: getting buy-in and building coalitions.
- Develop the dream.
- Nurture the working team.
- Master the difficult middles.
- Persist and persevere.
- Celebrate accomplishment.
- Make everyone a hero.

A raw idea that emerges from kaleidoscope thinking must be shaped into a theme that makes the idea come alive. Ideas do not launch productive changes until they become a theme around which others begin to improvise—a "Third Circle" that raises aspirations. There is a gap between dreaming and doing that is filled by the support of others. As I cautioned earlier, a "Third Circle" remains just a dream unless it is communicated and can inspire others to follow. Selling the "Third Circle" involves conveying the:

- Destination: where are we headed?
- Dream: what will be different because of this goal; what will our world look like then?
- Prize: what positive outcomes will be obtained?
- Target: what deadlines or metrics make the outcomes concrete?
- Message: what memorable image, slogan, or headline conveys the essence of the goal?
- First Step: what tangible step can be taken that will give reality to the goal? A journey of a thousand miles begins with a single step.

The "Third Circle" is more than a written goal that is distributed to people, like a business plan or a mission statement; rather, it is embodied in the change leader's personal enthusiasm and reflected in his or her passion. If a project is viewed as just another assignment, then either it is so routine that it does not produce much change, or skeptics and resisters have good reason not to go along with it. To make anything successful, you must work a personal network. Change leaders need the support of power holders. Effective coalition building relies on three kinds of action: pre-selling (speaking to many people, gathering intelligence, and planting a "seed"), making deals (getting others to chip in and getting a sanity check), and confirming or adjusting the idea in light of reactions from backers and potential backers.

Several common problems or saboteurs arise in the middle of developing new products, implementing new processes, or getting new ventures off the ground. They include:

- Forecasts fall short.
- The plan does not hold.
- Unexpected obstacles pop up.
- Panic ensues with unpredictable twists and turns.
- Momentum slows and the team gets tired.
- Critics get louder just at the point the initiative is most vulnerable.

A person's attitude toward a change tends to evolve as he or she becomes more familiar with the change. The stages a person goes through can consist of apprehension, denial, anger, resentment, depression, cognitive dissonance, compliance, acceptance, and internalization. It is management's job to create an environment in which people can go through these stages as quickly as possible and even skip some. Effective change management programs are frequently sequential, with early measures directed at overcoming the initial apprehension, denial, anger, and resentment, but gradually evolving into a program that supports compliance, acceptance, and internalization.

Resistance is a Natural Emotional Process

Resistance to change is a natural emotional process. But sometimes we disguise our emotional response with logic, and others experience us as demanding, ignorant, unreasoning, killing the messenger, deal-making, or secretive. The most effective counter to resistance is a "Third Circle" that describes so clearly what is possible combined with concrete steps to make the "Third Circle" a reality. Reflect on the following:

- When you last encountered resistance from someone, which fallback approach did you use?
- How did you react to the resistance (internally and externally)?
- What was the impact on the problem in the short-term? Did it lessen or increase the resistance? What was the impact in the long-term?
- What was the impact on your relationship with that person in the short-term? Long-term? What did they learn about how you respond to resistance?
- What, if anything, would you do differently next time?

As a leader or a colleague you need to provide non-judgmental listening. Validate the person exhibiting the resistance and acknowledge his or her reactions as "normal." Provide the opportunity for grievances and frustrations to be aired constructively. Also, consider appropriate resources and support that you can leverage, such as access to an employee assistance program.

People do not check their personal or family problems at the door when they reach the factory gate or the reception area. At any given time, any given number of employees may experience levels of stress that are high enough to distract them from their work and cause them to be less productive than they might otherwise be. Employers have no direct control over these issues, but it may be possible to deal with them through an employee assistance program.

Other problems, as the "prospective medicine" approach to organizational health reminds us, may be generated by culture and the organization of the workplace. In these situations, keep calm and respond non-defensively when others disagree with you. Develop creative and innovative solutions to problems and be willing to adjust priorities to changing conditions. Be open and candid when dealing with others, and be sure to participate actively in the change process.

Challenges for Today's Leaders

Today, there are some interesting challenges for leaders. For example, there is a shortage of competently prepared leaders. The baby-boomer pool upon which to draw is getting smaller. Often, factors that affect business cannot be predicted. For example, changes in interest rates, the price of petroleum or other commodities, downturns in the economy, global distress, and so on. Knowledge of demography, however, is knowledge of the future. We *know* that by the end of this decade, 40 percent of the workforce will be eligible for retirement—with that retirement, there will be a tremendous loss of institutional memory unless plans are put into place to preserve it. Similarly, these retirees will take with them knowledge that can be gained only through experience. They are leaving the workforce with knowledge that did not even exist two decades ago. This constitutes an unprecedented exodus in terms of numbers and in terms of knowledge. How are we going to deal with these issues?

Part of the answer must surely be the identification of talented younger employees who can be successfully mentored and sponsored for leadership positions. Yet many high potential leaders reject the stressful role. How can they be persuaded that both the challenges and rewards of leadership can be great and that the stress can be mitigated by a sense of perspective, balance, and the perception of being more in control of one's own destiny?

Many potential leaders cannot cope with the speed of change, but change is endemic and a permanent feature of the global economy. Others cannot handle the ambiguity and uncertainty of the role. It is as if they are trapped by a Newtonian view of the way the world operates, a view of the world in which the clockwork universe is linear, stable, and predictable. Similarly, their view of the world is one in which a small event has a proportionately small effect and a large event has a large effect. In the New Science (which is rooted in non-linearity) the universe is a much less predictable place in which small events can have enormous effects or no effects at all. The proportionality of cause and effect is undone.

Finally, Gandhi's challenge, "You must be the change you wish to see in the world," reminds me of what I call the algebra of relationships. When X equals Y; if we are X and we want Y to change, then Y is more apt to change if X changes. Understanding what that looks like is the challenge. Clearly, it will not happen without a healthy mental attitude toward change. Are you using the principles of positive psychology? Are you living your life with passion? Continuing the mathematical analogy, "Perpetual optimism," as Colin Powell asserts, "is a force multiplier."

Questions for Reflection

1. How have you responded to personal failures? What created resiliency for you? Were you able to learn from the experience?

2. How can you be adaptable and maintain your core values in life? How would you rate yourself in that regard?

3. What would inform you that you have a positive healthy mental attitude toward change?

4. Describe a time when you felt truly powerless in your life and felt that life was "happening to you." Reflecting back, did you have choices? Why or why not?

5. List three core values for you in the workplace. Think about a time when there was unwelcome change imposed in your career. What did you do to stay connected to your core values?

Chapter 10

Communicating Change

The problem with communication ... is the *illusion* that it has been accomplished.—*George Bernard Shaw*

Have you found your leadership voice? Can you sell the need for change? Can you lead your organization through the adversaries and resistances to change?

The majority of my corporate clients cite communication as their most challenging human factor issue. This is not surprising, given the logic of the **Paradigm**, since it depends on listening, respect, and knowing.

I will often listen all day to a leadership team that I am coaching as they discuss their business plan and, hopefully, its execution. At the end of the day, I offer observations about what I heard. Invariably, I am making observations about how the group communicated, or did not. Besides the **Paradigm-related** saboteurs, such as lack of listening or respect, the biggest obstacle was communication skills. In the course of the day there was so much noise but little connectivity.

When we use the word communicate, we are referring not only to the words one uses to transfer factual information to others, but also to other "messages" that are sent and received. In fact, experts estimate that 65 to 90 percent of what you communicate is nonverbal.

Verbal and Nonverbal Communication

Scholars in this field of verbal communication usually use the term "verbal" in the strict sense, meaning "of or concerned with words," and do not use "verbal communication" as a synonym for oral or spoken communication only. Thus, sign languages and writing are generally understood as forms of verbal communication. Nonverbal communication is usually understood as the process of sending and receiving wordless messages. Such messages can be communicated through gesture; body language or posture; facial expression and eye gaze; object communication such as clothing, hairstyles, or even architecture; symbols and info-graphics; and prosodic features of speech such as intonation and stress and other paralinguistic features of speech such as voice quality, emotion, and speaking style.

The Process of Communication

Communication is effective when a concise and clear message is delivered well, received successfully, and understood fully. The process of communication has the following distinct components:

- The sender/communicator
- The message
- The medium/channel choice

- The receiver/audience
- Feedback/response

Through words, actions, body language, voice tone, and other processes you send many messages about yourself, the changes, and your organization. This constitutes precisely one-half of the communication process. The second half consists of verifying that the message you intended to send was actually received and interpreted the way you intended. The only way that you can be sure you have created understanding is to listen to the people you are communicating with, and make special effort to encourage them to reflect back to you what they have heard, and what they make of it.

Remember that although you communicate in a way that seems clear to you, the receiver of the communication filters the information through a very complicated set of preconceptions that can function to distort the message received. Also, receivers listen selectively. They hear and process some things and gate out other things. That means that while you may have explained the "whole picture," it is not likely that the whole thing was received. To ensure that you have created common understanding within others, ask them what they have heard and what their reactions are to your message.

As a regular airplane traveler, I tend to be a selective listener and often disregard the messages from pilots, co-pilots, and flight attendants. Even with weather delays I am somewhat cynical about the veracity of what I am being told. One day, however, on a flight from Lexington, Kentucky to St. Louis, Missouri, the captain got my undivided attention. After a noticeably rapid descent, he came on the intercom and announced that there was a light on in the cockpit indicating smoke in the luggage hold at the rear of the small commuter aircraft.

Obviously trained for such contingencies, he explained that he could only tell us one time what the situation was and what the plan of action would be. He told us he was cleared directly into Louisville International Airport. He explained that once we landed, and came to a full stop, all kinds of safety equipment would surround the aircraft. The front door would be opened and the flight attendant would direct us down the steps on to the ground. We were told to leave all belongings behind us. Once on the ground, we were to assemble exactly where the ground staff directed us.

Fortunately, we landed safely, there was no fire, and we were reassigned to an alternate plane for the onward journey. Everything unfolded the way the captain had described down to the noise and smell as the wings of huge Boeing 747 cargo planes passed over our heads.

The captain broke our preoccupation. He was clear and concise and, like a parent taking a child to the dentist for the first time, described what it would feel like as we progressed through each stage of the potential crisis.

Unfortunately, some leaders believe that effective communication consists of memo sending or orally telling people what is going on, or what will happen. While the latter may work in a crisis situation, in the technological age, this becomes more of an issue. Whether it is sending an e-mail instead of creating dialogue or the substitution of PowerPoint slides instead of discussing issues, communication in the workplace has changed. Passing on information is only one part of communication. Communication can be simply described as creating understanding. In periods of change, as in "normal" times, the leader must not only pass information to employees, but also ensure that it is understood correctly. After all, the leader stands to lose a great deal if information is not understood, as he or she is accountable for the results.

So, keep in mind that communication must be two-way in manner, where the leader may be communicating to employees but is also soliciting comments from employees about their level of understanding and their level of comfort about potential changes. As a change leader you need to make decisions about whom you must communicate with, what needs to be communicated, when you will communicate, and how you will do it.

Leaders sometimes have a tendency to communicate about change on a "need-to-know basis." Effective change leaders recognize, however, that almost any change will have effects on most people in an organization, no matter how removed they are from the change. The basic rule of thumb is that communication should take place between the leader and the directly and indirectly affected employees, and/or when employees are inquisitive and want to know. Except where confidentiality is critical or where security clearances are required, you are better off over-including people in your communication rather than excluding people.

Communication Styles

While the content of a communication will vary, there are some guidelines to follow:

- Give information that will reduce uncertainty and ambiguity regarding the change.
- Preempt gossip and anticipate and reconcile anxiety about your change.
- Provide forums for employees to communicate their reactions and concerns to you.
- Use judgment when dealing with sensitive and confidential information.
- Create formal and informal modes of information transfer.

Choose the appropriate style to accomplish your communication objective, and the appropriate time. When you want the audience to learn from you, you will need to inform or explain, conveying something that you know but that they do not. You will want to persuade or advocate when you want your audience to change their thinking or behavior. When you want to learn from the audience, you can consult or brainstorm.

Historically, the communication channel choice was either writing (letter, memo, posted announcement) or speaking (to individuals, a group, in person, on phone). Now we have fax, e-mail, web pages, voice mail, electronic meetings, audio-conferencing, video-conferencing, and web casts. In the case of memo-writing versus e-mail, there could be the same or similar content, but writing a memo is seen as fairly reserved and controlled while e-mail is viewed as more informal, though preferences might be changing.

Group or Single Meetings

Another decision you need to address is what needs to be communicated in group settings, and what needs to be addressed in one-on-one meetings with employees. What are the advantages of each approach? Communicating in groups ensures that each person present is hearing the same information at the same time. Group communication also allows people to interact with each other about the changes and can help people develop a sense of team, particularly in a climate of adversity. Communicating in groups also has some disadvantages. In many organizations there are people who will not feel comfortable talking in a group context. The more "personal" the effects of the change; the more likely people will withdraw from the group process.

A second danger of group communication is that one or two particularly vocal and negative people can set the tone for the group and foster unproductive negative discussion. While expression of concern about a change is healthy, the "doomsayer" can cause this process to become destructive. For this reason, group communication needs to be managed with skill and expertise. Sometimes an external facilitator is necessary.

Finally, there are some issues that cannot be discussed within a group. For example, in downsizing situations it is inappropriate to announce to a group that John and Mary are losing their jobs. When changes are likely to create a high degree of upset to individuals, they must be dealt with in private. Communicating on a one-to-one basis has the advantage of privacy. When bad news is communicated, the person receiving the news is less pressured to withhold his or her reactions. One-to-one communication also allows more in-depth exploration of the person's feelings, ideas, and reactions to the change. A disadvantage to using one-to-one communication is that it may fragment your team. There is also a possibility that you will send slightly different messages to different staff members.

When to Use Written Versus Oral Communication

There is a tendency for leaders to avoid unpleasant interactions with employees and use written communication to avoid the discomfort of dealing face-to-face with staff. While written communication can play an important role in communicating about change, it should not be used for this purpose alone. Use oral communication when the receiver is not very interested in getting the message, emotions are high, you need feedback, the other person is too busy or preoccupied to read, you need to convince or persuade, or when the details and issues are complicated and cannot be well expressed on paper.

Written communication is more appropriate when you require a record of the communication for future reference; when your staff will be referring to details of the change later; or when you are communicating something with multiple parts or steps and it is important that employees understand them. Generally, it is wise to use both written and oral communication. The more emotional the issues, the more important it is to stress oral communication first. Written communication can be used as backup. Text only is the least rich channel, whereas text plus pictures plus voice plus body language is the most powerful channel.

There is no substitute for good judgment. Change leaders need to be reflective and thoughtful about the ways they communicate. There is also no substitute for listening and receiving feedback from your staff and colleagues about how you communicate. You may make communication mistakes, but the mark of an effective change leader is that these mistakes are quickly identified through feedback and discussion, and corrective action is taken.

Provide answers to questions only if you know the answers. Leaders destroy their credibility when they provide incorrect information or appear to stumble or back-pedal when providing an answer. It is much better to say you do not know, and that you will try to find out.

Leaders need to listen, just listen. Avoid defensiveness, excuse-making, and answers that are too quickly given. Act with thoughtfulness. The power of real listening cannot be overemphasized. Real listening is one of your most critical components in change communication. Make leaders and change sponsors available, daily when possible, to mingle with others in the workplace. Communication should be proactive.

An old proverb goes, "Every change brings an opportunity." In other words, we must learn to see change as a means of achieving our goals, not a barrier preventing us from reaching them. Another way of expressing the same thought is: a change in my external circumstances provides me with an opportunity to grow as a human being. The greater the change, the greater and faster I can grow. If we can perceive change along these lines, we will find it exciting and energizing, rather than depressing and debilitating.

Yet this restructuring of our perspective on change can take some time. In fact, coping with change follows the same steps as the grieving process. The steps are shock and denial that the old routine must be left behind, then anger that change is inevitable, then despair and a longing for the old ways, eventually replaced by acceptance of the new and a brighter view of the future. Everyone works through this process; for some, the transition is lightning fast; for others, painfully slow.

Lessons from the Battle of Agincourt

As a high school student in London, I was required to memorize many passages from the plays of William Shakespeare. To this day I can recite by heart King Henry V's famous speech in *Henry V*, Act III, Scene 1[1]. It has always struck me as a masterful example of communication preceded by listening, respect, and knowing—the foundation of the **Paradigm for Profitability**©.

The play is set in England and France in the early fifteenth century. The political situation in England is tense: King Henry IV has died, and his son, the young King Henry V, has just assumed the throne. Several bitter civil wars have left the people of England restless and dissatisfied. In order to gain the respect of the English people, Henry lays claim to certain parts of France based on his distant roots in the French royal family and on a very technical interpretation of ancient land laws.

When the young prince of France sends Henry an insulting message in response to these claims, Henry decides to invade France. Supported by the English noblemen and clergy, Henry gathers his troops and the English sail for France, where they fight their way across the country. The climax of the war comes at the famous Battle of Agincourt, at which the English are outnumbered by the French five to one.

The night before the battle, King Henry disguises himself as a common soldier and talks to many of the soldiers in his camp, learning who they are and what they think of the great battle in which they are about to fight. In essence, Henry was working the **Paradigm for Profitability**©, getting to know his soldiers, respecting and listening to their fears and self-doubts. He was then able to fashion a most inspiring solicitation for them to accept change and his vision. When Henry is by himself, he laments his ever-present responsibilities as king. On the morning of the battle, he prays to God and gives a powerful, inspiring speech to his soldiers. Miraculously, the English win the battle, and the proud French finally surrender. Henry's speech was as follows:

> Once more unto the breach, dear friends, once more;
> Or close the wall up with our English dead!
> In peace there's nothing so becomes a man
> As modest stillness and humility:
> But when the blast of war blows in our ears,
> Then imitate the action of the tiger;

> Stiffen the sinews, summon up the blood,
> Disguise fair nature with hard-favour'd rage;
> Then lend the eye a terrible aspect;
> Let it pry through the portage of the head
> Like the brass cannon; let the brow o'erwhelm it
> As fearfully as doth a galled rock

O'erhang and jutty his confounded base,

Swill'd with the wild and wasteful ocean.

Now set the teeth and stretch the nostril wide;

Hold hard the breath and bend up every spirit

To his full height!—On, on, you noblest English.

Whose blood is fet from fathers of war-proof!—

Fathers that, like so many Alexanders,

Have in these parts from morn till even fought,

And sheath'd their swords for lack of argument:—

Dishonour not your mothers; now attest

That those whom you call'd fathers did beget you!

Be copy now to men of grosser blood,

And teach them how to war!—And you, good yeoman,

Whose limbs were made in England, show us here

The mettle of your pasture; let us swear

That you are worth your breeding; which I doubt not;

For there is none of you so mean and base,

That hath not noble lustre in your eyes.

I see you stand like greyhounds in the slips,

Straining upon the start. The game's afoot:

Follow your spirit, and upon this charge

Cry—God for Harry! England!—and Saint George!

Reportedly, when King Abdullah II of Jordan ascended to the throne of the Hashemite Kingdom of Jordan in 1999 following the death of his father, King Hussein, he too, disguised himself and traveled among his citizens to listen to their fears and their frustrations with his government.

Houston, We Have a Problem!

Another powerful example of clear communication is exemplified by flight director Gene Kranz, played by actor Ed Harris, in Ron Howard's 1995 movie, *Apollo 13*[2]. Apollo 13 was the third manned lunar-landing mission and part of the United States Apollo program. It launched on April 11, 1970, with astronauts James A. Lovell, John L. Swigert, and Fred W. Haise. Two days after the launch, and 321,860 kilometers from Earth, the Apollo spacecraft was crippled by an explosion, causing the service module portion of the Apollo command/service module to lose its oxygen and electrical power. The crew used the lunar module as a "lifeboat" in space. The command module systems remained functional, but were deactivated to preserve their capability to re-enter Earth's atmosphere. The crew endured difficult conditions due to severe constraints on power, cabin heat, and potable water, but successfully returned to Earth.

In the movie there is a scene where chaos and confusion abound as the flight controllers at mission control in Houston confront the desperate reality of the situation onboard Apollo 13. Gene Kranz demands the attention of the group and proceeds to graphically illustrate on a wallboard the reality of what they are facing (the "First Circle"). He describes how the spacecraft developed the problem near the moon and how they decided to send the craft on a single pass around the moon and head back to Earth (the "Third Circle"). The free return trajectory used the moon's gravity to effectively "slingshot" the spacecraft back to Earth.

In a later scene he places a mark where the spacecraft currently is and declares that getting the crew back is non-negotiable and that it is his staff's job to figure out how to get the spacecraft from that point safely back to Earth (a new "Third Circle"). This was a challenge since the lunar module "lifeboat" was equipped to sustain only two people for two days. Instead it was required to sustain three people for four days.

With their noisy preoccupation broken, Kranz then focused the team on the problem and challenged them to use their creativity, as well as the creativity of the astronauts on board the spacecraft, to find a solution to their problem. The crew and the flight controllers showed considerable ingenuity under extreme pressure as they jury rigged the craft for the crew's safe return. This particular scene is a classic study in leadership, collaboration, and "followership." It is also an excellent study of problem-solving and ego strength.

"Ego" is frequently misunderstood, at least in the way that Freud intended. It is often confused with being "egotistical." Ego strength is best understood in terms of solving problems or dealing with frustrations. Persons high in ego strength tend to have a stoic mental orientation. They accept that effort, frustration, and loss are inevitable parts of life. They avoid unrealistic expectations. They formulate problems in concrete and specific terms and often reframe the problem in common-sense language. They also have an appropriate sense of timing, neither hurried nor slow-paced. They do not procrastinate. Nor do they try to comply with superhuman standards. They have positive self-images and can correctly discern the limits of their own control or responsibility. Finally, they prepare for stressful events by rehearsing for them.

Healthy problem-solvers pass through four stages. First, they stoically define the facts; second, they creatively explore all the options available to solve the problem; third, they select an option that does not create another problem; and fourth, they act upon their decision. Persons who are highly effective problem-solvers move through this sequence, almost imperceptibly. The confidence that results from this competence is ego strength. Reactive problem-solvers, in contrast, see only one option, do not like it, cannot make a decision, and cause chaos for others around them.

Gene Kranz demonstrated every aspect of healthy problem-solving while also working the **Paradigm** and the **Three Circles Model**© **for Change.**

"I'm in Control Here"

In contrast to Gene Kranz's authoritative communication skill, Alexander Haig, Jr., provided a classic example of how not to communicate in a crisis.

Coincidentally, I was in Washington, D.C., on March 30, 1981, the day that President Ronald Reagan was shot by John Hinckley, Jr., in an assassination attempt outside the Hilton Hotel. I was at a conference in the Sheraton Hotel just up the road. It was particularly eerie that night in the city. While the president was in the hospital having a bullet removed from his chest, Alexander Haig, his Secretary of State, asserted to reporters, "I'm in control here." Haig was exceeding his constitutional authority. Constitutionally, after the Vice President, it is the Speaker of the

House of Representatives and the President Pro Tem of the Senate who are in line of succession ahead of the Secretary of State.

A few years later, as I was taking the test to become a United States citizen, I was able to answer that particular question without hesitation.

The Importance of Dialogue

Dean Rusk, the United States Secretary of State under presidents John F. Kennedy and Lyndon B. Johnson, observed that "One of the best ways to persuade others is by listening to them."

With a similar message, Daniel Yankelovich, a public opinion analyst and social scientist, in his book *The Magic of Dialogue— Transforming Conflict into Cooperation*[3], stresses that dialogue is not debate, discussion, or deliberation. It has three core requirements: equality and the absence of coercive influences, listening with empathy, and bringing assumptions into the open. He reminds us that dialogue has tangible as well as intangible consequences, and we have to make dialogue happen.

Whether dealing in the international, corporate, or domestic realm we will have to give ground. Moreover, equality and empathy are necessary but not sufficient. We have to transform transactions into relationships. He also stresses that dialogue and decision-making do not mix.

Yankelovich suggests the following strategies for healthy dialogue:

1. Err on the side of including people who disagree with you.
2. Initiate dialogue through a gesture of empathy.
3. At the outset, check for the presence of all three core requirements of dialogue—equality, empathetic listening, and the surfacing of assumptions non-judgmentally, and learn how to introduce the missing ones.
4. Minimize the level of distrust before pursuing practical objectives.
5. Keep dialogue and decision making compartmentalized.
6. Focus on common interests, not divisive ones.
7. Use specific cases to raise general issues.
8. Bring forth your own assumptions before speculating on those of others.
9. Clarify assumptions that lead to subculture distortions.
10. Where applicable, identify mistrust as the real source of misunderstandings.
11. Expose old scripts to a reality check.
12. Focus on conflicts between value systems, not people.
13. Be sure trust exists before addressing transference distortions.
14. When appropriate, express the emotions that accompany strongly held values.
15. Encourage relationships in order to humanize transactions.

Even when the sole purpose of a dialogue is to reach a decision, the dialogue part of the process should precede the decision-making part. The line of demarcation between the two may be formal or informal, clear or vague, short or long. But the two must be kept separate or they will undermine each other. Most decisions do not, in fact, require dialogue, because a high level of mutual understanding among the decision makers is not usually needed. But for truly difficult decisions, the act of seeking mutual understanding through dialogue should come before all of the practical constraints and clash of interests involved in practical decision-making are brought to bear.

The 1998 Good Friday agreement[4], facilitated by Senator George J. Mitchell to resolve the conflict in Northern Ireland, is an example, close to my heart, of the potency of both dialogue and working the **Paradigm**.

Questions for Reflection

1. Are you afraid of the anger, fear, or grief of others? What can you point to in your life that supports your answer? Would others agree with your answer? Have you asked them?

2. Do you have a history of directly communicating change to those you have led? How did you deal with their fear?

3. List five things that people need in order to grow through challenging or threatening changes. Which of those things have you offered to help those you lead? What would you do differently based on previous experiences?

4. Take some time alone to imagine how your organization would look, sound, and operate on its absolutely best day. With this ideal in mind, take a walk through your organization. Beyond polite greetings, try not to engage

others too much; simply walk around and observe, listen, notice. How does what you see and hear compare to your "absolutely best day" images?

5. Stereotypically, men tend to process loss and grief more with their bodies and actions. Women are much better at processing feelings and thoughts via conversations with others in their support system. With that in mind, think about these questions: Is there something you can do that would help you to express or memorialize the loss? Is there someone you can talk to, who knows how to just listen, who would help? What would help you to embrace your past losses, bring them to a conscious level, so that you can "walk around them" and build a place for them?

Part V

Do You
Have the Will to Lead?

Chapter 11

Understanding Your Desire

The man who can drive himself further once the effort gets painful, is the man who will win.—*Roger Bannister*

Your feet will take you to where your heart is.

It is my experience that true leaders do not rest until their feet take them to their "Third Circle." The realization of the leader's dream is truly non-negotiable. Do you understand the desire underlying your will to lead?

Appreciation of the **Paradigm for Profitability**© and the **Three Circles Model**© **for Change** develops over time. As I said at the outset of this book, you do not become a leader through an injection. Invariably, after my clients obtain a mature understanding of the power of the **Paradigm** and the "Third Circle," they discreetly approach me with what they describe as a non-business related matter. Usually, it turns out to be their concern for a young adult child who does not have a "Third Circle." It is then that I know the executive "gets it."

How Do Children Learn to Walk?

I often ask participants in my seminars how they believe children learn to walk. Over the years I have heard all kinds of explanations. They put one foot in front of the other or they fall down and get up again. Invariably, the answers provide mechanical explanations. I believe that infants, to be sure, get upright and are perhaps supporting themselves against something. But, at the moment they launch themselves, they see someone or something they desire. It may be a parent inviting them to come to them or come and receive something. Regardless, they go out of balance, fall forward, but manage to find their footing. What they see at that moment is an infant version of a "Third Circle."

Roger Bannister's "Third Circle"

When we moved as a family from the Glens of Antrim to London, we settled first in the west London suburb of Hayes. I have so many vivid memories of that time. Unlike people in the Glens of Antrim, people in London did not readily greet one another on the street, and everyone seemed to wear dark clothes and ride black bicycles; not unlike what I see in China today. Bomb craters remained unfilled from the blitz on London, unexploded bombs were being discovered daily, and de-mobbed soldiers were still not fully assimilated back into the workforce or British society. It was a morbid, depressing, and foggy time.

But an incredible event soon after we arrived had the same impact on me as watching Neil Armstrong (a fellow Purdue Alum) land on the moon almost two decades later. It was Roger Bannister breaking the four-minute-mile barrier. That was he achieving his "Third Circle"—his feet taking him to where his heart was.

Roger Bannister was born in Harrow, a northwest suburb of London, also famous for Harrow Public School where Winston Churchill was a schoolboy, and where we had moved after Hayes and before I left for the University of London. As a youth, Bannister showed an exceptional talent for running. University education, however, was beyond the reach of Bannister's working class parents, so he resolved to win a place in one of England's elite universities and study medicine. At the outbreak of World War II, his family moved to historic Bath, in the West Country, where Roger had daily opportunities to practice his running on his way to and from school. At first, his studiousness made him unpopular with his less motivated classmates, but his exceptional speed on the running track soon earned him the acceptance he sought, and his scholastic efforts paid off with a scholarship to Oxford University.

At Oxford, Bannister's speed in the mile and 1,500-meter events drew the attention of the British sports press. To the consternation of many British track enthusiasts, the young miler declined to compete in the 1948 Olympics in London, preferring to concentrate on his training and his medical studies.

By 1951 Bannister had captured the British title in the mile and felt ready for Olympic competition. Unfortunately, a last minute change in the schedule of the events at the 1952 games in Helsinki forced Bannister to compete without resting between events as he was accustomed to. He finished fourth in the 1,500-meter run and endured the scorn of the British sports media, who blamed Bannister's rejection of conventional coaching and training methods.

Bannister resolved to redeem himself by breaking the world's record for the mile, the seemingly insurmountable four-minute barrier. By this time he had undertaken full-time medical studies, and could set aside only 45 minutes per day for training. But he had seen his time in the mile improve year after year, and was convinced that slow and steady training would enable him to break the record.

Bannister's opportunity came on May 6, 1954, in a meet at Oxford University, with Bannister competing for the British Amateur Athletic Association. He arranged for his friends Christopher Chataway and Chris Brasher to set the pace for the first three laps. He completed the first three quarter-mile laps in under three minutes. Finishing the last lap in less than a minute, Bannister broke the tape and collapsed as the announcer delivered his time to the cheering crowd: 3:59.4. The unbreakable record had been broken. At age 25, Roger Bannister had made history. The historic photograph of him crossing the finish line as the officials, including a minister, looked over the shoulder of the timekeeper is priceless. Roger Bannister completed his medical studies and for the next two decades combined a career in research with clinical practice as a neurologist.

There are many lessons in Sir Roger Bannister's achievement: the clarity of his "Third Circle," the unselfish trust and collaboration of his friends, the discipline to train and study at the same time, and the scientific approach that this pioneering exercise physiologist took to understanding how to withstand oxygen debt.

Essentially, understanding your desire is about uncovering your mature "Third Circle." A person is not entitled to the designation of "leader" if he or she does not have a "Third Circle," or cannot convincingly describe it. Moreover, it has to be more than a wish, a platitude, or a financial number.

There are two simple ways of classifying human purposes or one's desire to be a trusted and effective leader: competitive versus cooperative, and selfish versus unselfish. Whether in competitive/cooperative form or selfish/unselfish form, the general desire to achieve can be expressed in many ways throughout life. True leadership desire, or having the *will* to lead, is not about ambition or drive. Those can be very unhealthy motivations. Rather, it is about determination, resolve, and inspiration. Inspired people operate with or without rewards because they are driven internally by a sense of mission and purpose; that is, they are cooperative and selfless. Ambition, on the other hand, is typically about selfish and competitive individualism. This is one of the differences between a transformational and charismatic leader as against a narcissistic one.

The Desire to Survive

A few years ago I met someone who exemplified courage, survival, and leadership. I was dining at the St. Elmo—a popular steakhouse and Indianapolis institution. Seated next to me was an older couple. I asked what brought them to Indianapolis. "I am a survivor of the *U.S.S. Indianapolis* and am here for our 54-year reunion," the man said.

The gentleman gave me a fascinating history of the fate of the *Indianapolis*, a heavy cruiser. In particular, he told about the unsuccessful attempts by its survivors to have their skipper, Captain Charles Butler McVay III, exonerated of the guilty verdict in his court-martial following the torpedoing of his ship by a Japanese submarine on July 30, 1945. The Navy convicted him of "hazarding his vessel by failing to zigzag."

The *Indianapolis* had delivered the atom bomb to Tinian Island in the Marianas two days earlier. My new acquaintance had gone on watch literally minutes before the *Indianapolis* was attacked. The ship sank within 12 minutes. Of an original complement of 1,280 men approximately 800 did not go down with the ship. He spent five days floating in shark-infested waters. He was one of 317 who were not eaten by sharks or did not die from exposure.

Since the survivors now totaled only about 50, I asked who would keep up the pressure on the Department of the Navy. He explained that the survivors have a "Second Watch" consisting of grandchildren and younger relatives. Despite all their efforts, the captain of the *Indianapolis* committed suicide in 1968.

My new acquaintance was clearly enjoying life and was passionate about the mission that he and the other survivors of the *Indianapolis* have set for themselves. As we got up to leave the table I asked him what age he was when he floated for five days and no one was even looking for him. "Nineteen" he said. I do not know if he had a "Third Circle" at that time. He certainly did when I met him.

Questions for Reflection

1. What is your "Third Circle?"
2. In order of importance, list five things that motivate you toward your goals.
3. Which creates more lasting change, something positive coming into your life or pain?
4. List five longings in your life. Which of those can you realistically acquire without the help of others, and which will require the help of others?
5. Walk through your home. Imagine you have a wheelbarrow. What would you keep from your home if all you could keep could be taken only in the wheelbarrow? Make a list of what you choose and why? List how that represents a lasting desire or value for you?

Chapter 12

Understanding Your Ambition

People seem not to see that their opinion of the world is also a confession of character.—*Ralph Waldo Emerson*

What fuels your ambition? What will you do to get ahead in business? As Emerson's quote confirms; so much of what we do is a confession of our character. The true measure of a man, the famous quote goes, is how he treats someone who can do him absolutely no good. In fact, unhealthy ambition can be one of the greatest saboteurs to achieving our personal or professional "Third Circle."

If you look up the word *ambition* in the dictionary, you will find it described as an ardent desire for rank, fame, or power; a desire to achieve a particular end or a strong desire for advancement. Ambition in the corporate world applies to the persistent demand for personal advancement or preferment and may suggest an ardent longing for recognition of accomplishment. This can often occur without actual possession of the necessary abilities and, therefore, implies presumption or pretentiousness.

Does this mean that true leaders do not have aspirations or do not strive for something higher than oneself? No, psychologists agree that pursing growth and mastery is essential for well-being. The line between ambition and will, however, is subtle. Knowing oneself, owning the leadership role, and, most importantly, having a "Third Circle" guided by strong values and principles will reveal a will to lead that extends beyond avarice. Essentially, the distinguishing factor that is the dividing line between ambition and will is motivation.

This may be an appropriate time to revisit the questions regarding your life's story and the myths with which you were raised. Whose voice do you hear encouraging you to assume a leadership role? Is it your parents'? Is it your spouse's? What are their motives?

In my consulting work I am amazed by how many executives live in a constant state of fear with all the associated health and medical consequences. This can be a fear of failure or a fear of success. It is a fact that the underbelly of the need to dominate is fear. Such dominance is a guaranteed saboteur to the true ownership of the **Paradigm** and the ability to live with passion and lead through trust.

Scientists Eventually Become Philosophers

It is a truth that scientists end up philosophers, for they cannot disconnect the power of their creations from their application to the good of mankind. It is for the same reason that true leaders aspire to understand and protect the soul of their business. That is why the most revealing question I pose to my clients and help them articulate the answer is: "What is the soul of your business?"

If you can answer that question with conviction and inspiration, you will have significantly progressed toward being a trusted and effective leader. But it is a lifelong process and can be a very lonely journey. That is why mentoring and executive coaching can be a powerful support that guides you to your vision.

Unfortunately, it is my observation that many people in today's culture may have a "Third Circle" but have a very difficult time identifying what it is. Either they have been told that thinking such thoughts is superfluous or navel gazing and as a consequence unproductive or too "touchy feely." So they do not engage in conversations with others about this, nor do they allow themselves to think in such terms. This is tragic.

For too long, the striving seen in entrepreneurs has been misunderstood as selfishness or egomania. This is perhaps true in those who succumb to a twisted view of reality, whose "Third Circle" has been distorted by a certain degree of selfishness or personality disorder. There is often a thin line between madness and genius. But there is, within the heart of humankind, something heroic. It seeks an outlet and hears a call.

We also have a universal need for communal reciprocity. This experiential encounter was called peak experience and self-actualization by psychologist Abraham Maslow. Henri Nouwen[1], a Catholic priest and psychologist, called it Holy Ground in his book *Reaching Out.* Jewish mystic Martin Buber[2] wrote in his book *I and Thou* that relation is reciprocity, and he called it the encounter of the "I" and "Thou." As humans, we are hard-wired to strive for superiority, and it is the one who strains his or her neck for the view from the highest point who shapes culture and identifies potential. I believe that the theories and suggestions in this book can lead those who seek that view to develop intentionally, and with measurable discipline.

Keeping Your Word

Carolyn Woo, Dean of the Mendoza College of Business at The University of Notre Dame, is committed to the utmost integrity in business relations since it is the foundation of trusted and effective leadership. Not long ago she wrote a letter to *The Wall Street Journal* describing an encounter she had with one of her students[3]. When the student reneged on a job offer she had accepted, Dean Woo was deeply disappointed. She acknowledged that there were many reasons, all enticing, but none acceptable. The student could not reverse what she had done, but Dean Woo believed that a message had to be sent to the employer, the student, and the student body.

She arranged for a conference call to the employer to convey her deep apologies. She asked that the student be present to witness the exchange. Dean Woo believed that it was important that the student know her action compromised the college. She also wanted her to see a public apology in action.

In her letter Dean Woo wrote, "We know success in the business world requires persistence, drive and the desire to excel. On the other hand, we must be careful that these traits don't lead to self-absorbed, ungenerous behavior." In her letter she exposed the unhealthy aspects of competition. "Competition," she noted, "has its appropriate place. It gives us discipline, focus and a sense of accomplishment. At the macro level, open and competitive markets work. Competition engenders efficiency and accountability. What's cause for concern is that we're often competitive when the situation doesn't call for it."

She lamented the lack of true and healthy collaboration, and, paraphrasing her, in my language, ownership of the **Paradigm**. If the young woman did not learn from Dean Woo's lesson, it is hard to imagine that she will be able to establish trust with her employees, customers, or shareholders.

Can You Hear the Music?

"No one can whistle a symphony," said Halford E. Luccock, "it takes an orchestra to play it." My colleague Fintan Muldoon also has an excellent metaphor for this topic. He is a co-facilitator with me in the seminar *Trusted and Effective Leadership— Reclaiming the Creativity to Lead Change*, which we typically conduct at Ballynahinch Castle in the West of Ireland. He relates his daughter Emily's experience as a symphony orchestra oboist. Regardless of the charisma of the conductor, or the ambition of individual musicians, when the music starts, it is the music that leads and that the orchestra members follow. It is the music, as "Third Circle," that takes precedence. Can you hear the music of your "Third Circle?"

Questions for Reflection

1. Recall a time you wanted to give up and quit, but did not. What made the difference for you?

2. If someone who truly knows you carved the epitaph on your tombstone; what would it say if it spoke the truth about who you are? Does that reflect what you would like it to say?

3. List four attributes that differentiate longing for versus realizing your ambition. Which of those do you have? Rank them in order of importance.

4. If you knew you were going to drop dead in 90 days, how would you spend your remaining time? Give yourself three minutes to answer this question by jotting down as many quick answers as you can. Don't get sidetracked by life insurance or getting your affairs in order. (This idea is from Alan Lakein's book *How to Get Control of Your Time and Your Life*[4].)

5. Write down three principles that guide your ambitions. Write one page on each of those guiding principles in your life. Include events from your past that created those ambitions.

Chapter 13

Guiding Your Vision

Your vision will become clear only when you look into your heart. Who looks outside, dreams. Who looks inside, awakens.—*Carl Jung*

Who is guiding your vision? Who helps you stay focused on your "Third Circle?" Who helps you recalibrate your personal and professional life when everything around you is changing?

The Importance of Mentoring

Clearly, vital and creative leaders willingly receive and provide mentoring and executive coaching. In its simplest form, mentoring is a relationship between two people, one with greater experience (the mentor) who guides an individual with lesser experience (the protégé) to a higher level of personal and professional excellence. Mentoring has been called a high level of consciousness-raising. The "fist" mentor was the goddess Athena (the goddess of wisdom) who mentored Odysseus as well as his son Telemachus.

There are a variety of roles that mentors can play: *sponsor* (widens the exposure of the protégé); *teacher* (creates learning opportunities for the protégé); *devil's advocate* (challenges and confronts the protégé in order to help the protégé practice asserting ideas and influencing a listener who is higher up in the organization); and *coach* (supports the protégé by finding out what is important to him or her—for example, skills, aspirations, and interests). Mentoring can and should involve helping the subordinate with his or her current job performance and personal and professional developmental needs, and provide guidance to achieve goals at various career levels.

Mentoring should not be confused, however, with coaching or counseling. One distinction is that mentoring is more open-ended and less goal-directed than coaching or counseling. Another distinguishing feature is that mentors are not necessarily formally contracted. Their participation is generally voluntary, and their time is not compensated for monetarily. Rather, mutual growth for both the mentor and the protégé is the reward for mentoring.

Why Mentor?

Being a mentor can help enhance your skills as a leader as well as turn you into more of an asset to the organization. Mentoring is a critical skill for present executives and leaders of organizations to possess, as they are partially responsible for the training and development of future leaders. That is, mentoring enables organizations to develop and retain talent. Further, by passing on its values and mission to the protégé, the organization ensures the continuation of its legacy. Typically, mentoring can be accomplished in the confines of the organization; coaching, in contrast, requires a certain safety and objectivity that an external coach can provide.

Who Mentors Whom?

A mentor is an experienced, objective yet empathetic sounding board with the power to influence events. A mentor should take pride in his or her organization, relish new challenges, and understand and support the mission, vision, and values of the organization. Often, mentors identify with the dreams and aspirations of their protégés. It is crucial that mentors be respected within the organization, be knowledgeable in their job, have good professional skills, and have a collaborative spirit and well-defined organizational values.

Two major distinguishing factors for mentoring are the authority of the mentor and the mentor's ability to "sound the horn" for the protégé within the organization. In addition to being powerful, knowledgeable people within their organizations, mentors should be willing to share their expertise and not be threatened by the protégé's potential for equaling or even surpassing them. That is, the mentor should be someone who enjoys seeing others become accomplished. A caution: the mentor should not be someone to whom the protégé directly reports. This is because a protégé should feel that he or she can express his or her fears, frustrations, and goals without fear of reprisal from the mentor.

The protégé is a person who voluntarily seeks someone with greater experience and wisdom to help guide him or her through the maze of life, show him or her what doors to open, and help him or her learn the ropes of the organization. The protégé should have the ability and willingness to assume responsibility for his or her professional growth and development.

The Mentoring Process

Most important to the mentoring process is the presence of trust in the mentoring relationship. In order to establish trust, mentoring, much like being a trusted and effective leader, requires close attention to the **Paradigm for Profitability**©.

As mentioned above, mentors *know* themselves, their business, and the organization's vision for the future. Additionally, mentors must *know* their protégé (hopes, dreams, strengths, weaknesses, etc.). Next, mutual *respect* is an important aspect of the mentoring relationship. This is established in part by the shared values and vision that most mentors and protégés possess; where the protégé differs from the mentor, however, the difference must be acknowledged and honored. Quality *communication* between the protégé and the mentor begins with the mentor's willingness to *listen* to the protégé's needs and concerns. Through quality communication, an effective mentoring *relationship* can begin.

With the establishment of trust through successful navigation of the **Paradigm for Profitability**©, the next step is to create focus for the protégé. Having specific professional development objectives in place will allow for the creation of learning experiences that relate directly to the protégé's developmental needs and goals. To ensure a powerful learning experience, tasks should challenge but not overwhelm the protégé. Further, it is thought that protégés learn best in mentoring relationships that entail trial and error and observation. For this reason, mentors should provide opportunities for protégés to observe and participate in their work. Meetings should be scheduled to review progress on stated objectives as well as to assess satisfaction and fit of the relationship.

Some Cautions

The mentoring relationship is designed to help protégés with job-related matters or career issues; it is not an occasion to discuss personal problems. Therefore, the relationship must be exclusively professional and maintain professional boundaries. This means not soliciting or responding to personal issues as well as respecting each other's time and professional responsibilities. This also includes recognizing that not all suggestions, advice, or recommendations will be heeded, given that decisions impact the protégé and will ultimately be made based on what he or she feels is in his or her best interest. With the proper establishment of trust, through knowing, respecting, listening, and communication, both parties will be able to ensure that a quality professional relationship is maintained.

Both the mentor and the protégé should be prepared to take on their respective roles. They should not be thrown into the situation in the hope that there will be a baptism by fire that actually works.

Do you have a mentor? Do you mentor others?

Executive Coaching

It has been suggested that in the corporate world today, the sign that an executive has "made it" is to have an executive coach. Executive coaching is not, however, just a passing trend.

Evidence for this lies in research indicating that executive coaching produces appreciable results. Indeed, a great deal has been written about executive coaching, including what it is, why it is important, and steps that must be taken for successful coaching.

What Is Executive Coaching?

Executive coaches are considered the new strategic resource utilized by leaders in order to succeed in today's exceedingly complex global business world. By definition, a coach is a person who gives honest feedback and support, inspires others, challenges, facilitates growth and change, and partners with another person to achieve stated goals. An executive coach focuses on the goals and development of the executive in a context that has high performance expectations.

Executive coaches are the strategic partners who help unleash or reclaim the creativity to lead change. They shadow the leader's behavior and suggest changes that will help the leader create a healthy organization. An executive coach guides others through the very contents of this book. They are the vehicle for an executive's reflection and learning and for putting that learning into action to improve both himself or herself and his or her organization.

Executive coaching can take the form of executive role development, executive skill building, personal transition, problem solving, and career counseling. In truth, however, the majority of executive coaches are hired primarily to help executives hone their people skills as opposed to their business skills. This makes sense when considering that executives did not reach the top by failing to meet their numbers. Ironically, it is their position of power that precludes them from receiving feedback regarding behavioral habits, attitudes, traits, and the interpersonal skills that result in true *profitability*. For this reason, personal development is the cornerstone of executive coaching. A fundamental element of the coaching process is that the coach guides the leader in how to make self-development a fixture in the ever more challenging world of the executive leader. Ultimately, the executive coach empowers the leader to develop a greater sense of control in his or her personal as well as professional life.

The Executive Coaching Process

It is difficult to describe the executive coaching process, because there are as many methods and techniques as there are executive coaches. In general, however, there are three phases in the coaching process. The first of these is *contracting*, in which the client and the coach discuss goals, estimated resources, time commitment, potential methods, and cost. The next step is the *data collection* phase, in which the coach performs assessments and gathers feedback. Finally, the third phase is the true *coaching* phase, during which the coach and the client analyze the results of the data and design a plan of action to meet identified goals.

Essentially, the executive coaching process begins with the formation of a relationship between the executive and the coach. This relationship must involve respect on both sides and is significant, given that an executive coach's role is not just that of "cheerleader," but one in which the coach must challenge, probe, and confront the executive throughout the process. The next step in the process is to work toward expansion of the executive's self-awareness. In a sense, the executive coach exposes the client's blind spots and helps him or her to develop a mindfulness of his or her strengths and weaknesses. This helps the client to have a better understanding of his or her personal leadership style and how this may affect others.

With this increased awareness, the executive and the coach establish goals and a plan to achieve them. In order to achieve these goals, a fundamental mechanism for executive coaching is the use of feedback. The particular feedback gathered and reported will depend on the particular coach; studies have shown, however, that feedback from multiple sources within multiple levels of the leader's personal and professional life is most effective. Lastly, the coach enables the leader to seek out and fulfill opportunities for renewal and growth throughout his career.

Does Executive Coaching Work?

Change is difficult at any developmental or career stage; successful adults are unlikely to change, however, unless they have tremendous pressure and the tools and reinforcement with which to do so. It follows that executives utilizing coaches at key career points to provide the tools and reinforcement should be setting themselves up for successful learning and adaptation. Research supports this supposition both qualitatively and quantitatively. Qualitatively there have been countless articles that detail the testimonies of top executives who extol the virtues of executive coaching in terms of increasing humility, self-awareness, balance, focus, collaboration, accountability, and effectiveness. Affirmation can also be found in the fact that companies such as IBM spend more than $1.1 billion a year on training and leadership development. While this kind of proof is reassuring, there is a need for hard numbers to justify the often large monetary and time commitments required for executive coaching. To this end there exist several empirical studies supporting the usefulness of executive coaching for both the individual executive and the organization.

In terms of empirical data at the individual level, a study conducted by the International Coach Federation confirms that respondents report significant improvement in the following categories: self-awareness, goal setting, balancing life, stress levels, confidence, quality of life, communication skills, project completion, and relationships with co-workers. These factors contribute to a better work environment and subsequently increased effectiveness, productivity, and profitability because personal growth and corporate growth are intertwined.

Corroborating this at the organizational level is emerging empirical evidence that executive coaching provides company-wide benefits. For example, studies have established that executive coaching can enhance business performance and decrease overall production costs[1]. Additionally, executive coaching has been shown to dramatically increase creativity and problem solving, which has resulted in increased performance for both the executive and the organization. The payoff does not stop there; results suggest that when organizational performance increases, the result is better employee morale, increased customer satisfaction, increased market share, and increased profits. Finally, it has been shown that executive coaching has resulted in a 60 percent increase in leadership effectiveness (as perceived by others) when feedback has involved the use of a 360-degree feedback instrument[2]. This is primarily due to the need for executives to develop emotional intelligence (EI).

Emotional Intelligence

Indeed, EI has been found to be the differentiating factor for success; that is, 90 percent of the difference between outstanding and average leaders is linked to emotional intelligence[3]. EI is described as "the capacity for recognizing our own feelings and those of others, for motivating ourselves, and for managing emotions in ourselves and others[3]." In order for clients to realize EI, they must go through several levels of insight into their own behavior. At first, the client must be held accountable for his behavior. Next, the governing variables, norms, values, and limits of behavior must be considered in relation to the way he behaves. This helps the individual to see himself as operating within a "system," and further, to recognize that he or she does not have to be a puppet to these governing variables. Rather, through gaining insight and objectivity, the individual can begin to see how these variables shape his or her behavior while also distinguishing what he or she can and cannot control in terms of behavior.

How does an executive coach move an individual toward greater EI and greater awareness? There are countless books and articles detailing various methods and techniques. Clearly, what executives need most is to hone their "people skills," that is, the interpersonal skills of knowing, listening, communication, and relationship building. In other words, own the **Paradigm**.

It is said that such honing is arrived at only after the client is grounded in awareness of self and of others. These skills are not taught in graduate school but are essential to good business. Because human factors cannot be separated from the professional world, executives need assessments and comprehensive feedback specifically designed to ensure that they understand what is driving their behavior, how behaviors have and have not served them over the years, and how to enhance the human factors essential to leading a profitable business.

Foundation of Effective Coaching Programs

I believe that the most effective coaching programs are based on the principles of the **Three Circles Model© for Change** and the **Paradigm for Profitability©**. Effective leaders are aware of the pain or desire within themselves, within their workgroup, and within the organization as a whole. They recognize when there is a need for adjustment or growth. In order to move from the "First Circle" (pain/desire) through the "Second Circle" (insight/planning) to the "Third Circle" (shared vision) to create lasting change, the effective leader must have the competency to successfully navigate the **Paradigm for Profitability©**.

As I illustrated in earlier chapters, the **Paradigm for Profitability©** is a scientifically based model that represents the essential human factor elements that are preconditions for the development of trust within the organization and ultimately, true profitability. The model begins with both *knowing* oneself and *knowing* another. In terms of knowing oneself, the **Paradigm** emphasizes that effective and trusted leaders have awareness of their own beliefs, attitudes, and cognitions and display a high degree of intuition. Equipped with self-knowledge, the leader then has the self-initiative, interpersonal empathy, and emotional intelligence to move up the **Paradigm**. In terms of knowing the other, when employees feel known, they are not only happier but also more productive. Therefore, the **Paradigm** underscores the need for the effective and trusted leader to know his or her employees on a personal and professional level, including their strengths, weaknesses, goals, and career aspirations.

The next level of the **Paradigm** is *respect*. Respect allows for consciousness-raising, a sense of community, shared power, and inclusion. Accordingly, within the **Paradigm**, an effective and trusted leader demonstrates respect through recognition and appreciation of differences.

As we progress up the **Paradigm**, the human factor elements of *listening* and *communication* are highlighted. Through listening we give individuals the space to articulate their ideas and concerns, which allows us to understand the other's perspective. Listening conveys that we value the other's unique input and enables an individual to become a skillful conversationalist, to inquire about topics that are of importance to employees, and to convey a message of caring. The **Paradigm** maintains that executives must display the human factor of listening in order to be effective communicators.

Communication is delineated as more than just the content of our language; rather, the skill underscored in the **Paradigm** is communication competence, which refers to the "effectiveness" (degree to which communicators accomplish their goals in a communicative interaction) and "appropriateness" (degree to which interaction goals are achieved in a socially acceptable manner[4]).

Essential to completing the foundational portion of the **Paradigm** are building and maintaining *relationships* within the workplace, in which workers feel known, respected, and valued. When leaders demonstrate the ability to cultivate and maintain strong relationships with employees and customers, based on mutual understanding and trust, the precursors of *effectiveness, productivity, and profitability* are put in place.

Reclaiming the Creativity to Lead Change

Abraham Maslow wrote, "Musicians must make music, artists must paint, and poets must write if they are to be ultimately at peace with themselves. What human beings can be, they must be. They must be true to their own nature."

For over 15 years, I have been providing the executives I coach with an opportunity to stand back, reflect, and regain the creativity and energy to live with passion and lead through trust. My seminar *Trusted and Effective Leadership—Reclaiming the Creativity to Lead Change* allows my clients to redefine and reinvent their leadership presence.

In my work with organizations I essentially deal with three factors. First is the ubiquitous role of trust, upward, sideways, and downward. Second is the profound impact of stress on personal and organizational health. Third is the absence of a "Third Circle." This unique seminar addresses such topics as the pace of change in the workplace, loss of creativity, the evolving challenges of leadership, the roots of increased workplace stress, and other fundamental questions related to life and leadership. All executives face these issues at some point during their career. The more fortunate realize that continued success requires them to periodically address these and other issues.

Finally, as you reflect on your mentors and teachers, the people who asked you the essential leadership questions, I would like to share with you a poem by Séamus Heaney. He was born in the same part of Ireland as I. He won the 1995 Nobel Prize for Literature. This poem, *"Digging*[5]*,"* reflects his respect for his father's and his grandfather's skill at digging for turf. It also recognizes his appreciation of his life's story, what he and his ancestors stood for, and his realization of what he could do exceptionally well.

> Between my finger and my thumb
> The squat pen rests; snug as a gun.
> Under my window, a clean rasping sound
> When the blade sinks into gravelly ground:
> My father, digging. I look down
> Till his straining rump among the flowerbeds
> Bends low, comes up twenty years away
> Stooping in rhythm through potato drills
> Where he was digging
> The coarse boot nestled on the lug, the shaft

Against the inside knee was levered firmly.
He rooted out tall tops, buried the bright edge deep
To scatter new potatoes that he picked
Loving their cool hardness in our hands.
By God, the old man could handle a spade.
Just like his old man.

My grandfather cut more turf in a day
Than any other man on Toner's bog.
Once I carried him milk in a bottle
Corked sloppily with paper. He straightened up
To drink it, then fell to right away
Nicking and slicing neatly, heaving sods
Over his shoulder, going down and down
For the good turf. Digging.

The cold smell of potato mould, the squelch and slap
Of soggy peat, the curt cuts of an edge
Through living roots awaken in my head.
But I've no spade to follow men like them.

Between my finger and my thumb
The squat pen rests.
I'll dig with it.

With what will you dig?

Questions for Reflection

1. What is the essence of your "Third Circle?

2. How has your vision of what is important in life changed during your adult life?

3. Name three people with whom you share a vision. If they failed or quit in the pursuit of their vision, how did that impact you?

4. Do you currently have a mentor, coach, teacher, or accountability partner in your life? How might that be beneficial to you?

5. Who do you want to be during the last five years of your life?

Epilogue

Profitability, in the mature sense of the word, is more than a financial criterion. I hope that this book has expanded your definition of profitability to include those seldom tracked or measured elements of profitability, yet measures of a leader nonetheless. As you embark on your leadership career, or if you are in the process of reclaiming the creativity with which to lead, permit me to emphasize the importance of a few of the most critical human factors impacting your ability to live with passion and lead through trust.

First, reconnect with your life's story. In the words of the legendary Chinese philosopher Lao-tzu, "He who knows others is wise; he who knows himself is enlightened." Do not let others define you, but do listen carefully to how you are being experienced by others. You must be competent, but remember, leaders own the whole **Paradigm**. They are whole persons living with passion and leading through trust. Have you moved beyond a simple understanding of what personally drives you to a genuine self-awareness? Only people who truly know themselves can make others feel safe.

Second, acknowledge that without emotional safeness there is little hope for the execution of a theoretically elegant business plan. Shame on you if, intellectually, you agree with everything espoused in this book but are spineless when it comes to describing your "First Circle" and declaring your "Third Circle." You will be judged by what you finish, not by what you start.

Third, ensure that you belong to a healthy community and be careful with whom you associate. This applies to all domains of your life, such as your family, your neighborhood, your spiritual community, your social networks, and your workplace. If you accept the notion that people express their *soul* through their creativity and that the venue for that expression is the workplace, then you, as leader, have an awesome responsibility to create the kind of community that fosters safeness and permits the expression of innovation and creativity. Associate only with people who can and do support you in these endeavors. Do not associate with negative or self-centered people who have no concept of a "Third Circle."

Fourth, recognize that there is a tremendous loss of credibility in today's workplace, mainly due to a diminished trust in leaders. You are being watched and judged as to your integrity, competence, selflessness, and commitment. Are you greedy, disrespectful, opportunistic, and shallow? Or, do you serve as a positive role model with the passion and personal energy you expect of others throughout your organization?

Fifth, confront the unhealthy impact of stress. Take care of yourself. Tal Ben-Shahar[2], an author in the field of positive psychology, notes in his book, *"Happier,"* that the key to happiness is the combination of doing meaningful work that is also pleasurable. That combination results in true enjoyment.

Sixth, remove the opaqueness and lack of hope surrounding your own and your organization's "Third Circle." Only those who live with passion and lead through trust can reach their "Third Circle" and be able to help others to reach theirs. I have never forgotten the parting words from the president of the college from which I graduated at the University of London. He reminisced that college days were golden days with the safeness to gain new knowledge, explore outrageous ideas, and most importantly, develop our dreams. But he cautioned us that there would be people who would trivialize the potential, or refute the credibility, of our dreams as well as our strategies to reach them. He admonished us to uncompromisingly retain the passion for our dreams, but be ready to deal with those who, out of their own fears, would overtly or inadvertently attempt to sabotage our well-intentioned efforts.

Lastly, acknowledge that every leader will, at some time in his life, have his back against the wall. I hope that when that day comes for you, you can recalibrate, re-energize, and use what you have learned from your study of my five essential leadership questions to live with passion and lead through trust.

Be not afraid. As the narrator in Andrew Lloyd Webber's stage play and movie *Joseph and the Amazing Technicolor Dreamcoat* whispers to the audience, regarding Joseph's imprisonment, "I have read the book; I know how it ends."

I predict that your adversaries, whether passive or aggressive, do not have a system to defeat you. So, remember, no one cares more about your life, your personal affairs, or your destiny than you do.

Work the **Paradigm**, pursue your "Third Circle," and protect your *soul* and the *soul* of your enterprise.

End Notes

Prologue
1. Abraham H. Maslow, *Motivation and Personality*, Harper and Row, 1970.

Chapter 1: Drawing From Your Life's Story
1. Erik Erikson, *Identity and the Life Cycle*, International Universities Press, 1959.
2. Marcia Emery, *Intuition Workbook: An Expert's Guide to Unlocking the Wisdom of Your Subconscious Mind*, Prentice-Hall, 1994.

Chapter 2: Standing for Something
1. S. Truett Cathy, *It's Easier to Succeed than to Fail*, Oliver-Nelson, 1989.
2. John O'Donohue, *Anam Cara: A Book of Celtic Wisdom*, Harper Collins, 1997.
3. Ernst F. Schumacher, *Small Is Beautiful: Economics as if People Mattered*, Perennial Library, 1973.
4. The Framingham Heart Study is a cardiovascular study based in Framingham, Massachusetts. The study began in 1948 with 5,209 adult subjects from Framingham, and is currently in its third generation of participants. Most of the now common knowledge concerning heart disease, such as the effects of diet, exercise, and common medications such as aspirin, is based on this longitudinal study. Since 1971 it has been a project of the National Heart, Lung, and Blood Institute, in collaboration with Boston University. Various health professionals from the hospitals and universities of greater Boston staff the project.

5. The Society of Prospective Medicine is now part of the Research and Development Center, a division of the Institute for Health and Productivity Management, Scottsdale, AZ.

Chapter 3: Being Exceptional

1. Barry R. Schlenker, Beth A. Pontari and Andrew N. Christopher, "Excuses and Character: Personal and Social Implications of Excuses," *Personality and Social Psychology Review*, 2001.
2. Avshalom Caspi and Brent W. Roberts, "Personality Development Across the Life Course: The Argument for Change and Continuity," *Psychological Inquiry*, 2001.
3. A. Howard and D. W. Bray, *Managerial Lives in Transition*, Guilford Press, 1988.
4. Georgia T. Chao, Patm Walz and Philip D. Gardner, "Formal and Informal Mentorship: A Comparison on Mentoring Functions and Contrast with Nonmentored Counterparts," *Personnel Psychology*, 1992.
5. Phillip Hanson, *"The Johari Window: A Model for Soliciting and Giving Feedback."* In John E. Jones and William J. Pfeiffer, Eds., *The 1973 Annual Handbook for Group Facilitators*. University Associates, Inc., 1973.

Chapter 4: Making People Feel Safe

1. John O'Donohue, *Anam Cara: A Book of Celtic Wisdom*, Harper Collins, 1997.
2. Richard Gillespie, *Manufacturing Knowledge: A History of the Hawthorne Experiments*, Cambridge University Press, 1991.
3. Stanley Schachter, "Non-Psychological Explanations of Behavior." In L. Festinger, Ed., *Retrospections on Social Psychology*, Oxford University Press, 1980.
4. Rick Warren, *The Purpose Driven Life: What on Earth Am I Here For?* Inspirio, 2003.

Chapter 5: Knowing What Attracts Others to Follow You

1. Noel Coward, *Blythe Spirit*, Samuel French, 1941.
2. John B. Keane, *Moll*, Mercier Press, 1991.

Chapter 6: Building Relationships Based on Trust

1. The Society of Prospective Medicine is now part of the Institute for Health and Productivity Management (IHPM), Scottsdale, AZ.
2. Constantine Andriopoulos, "Determinants of Organisational Creativity: A Literature Review," *Management Decision*, 2001.

Chapter 7: Sustaining Trust

1. Viktor E. Frankl, *Man's Search for Meaning*, Beacon Press, 1959.
2. Elizabeth Kübler-Ross, *On Death and Dying*, Touchstone, 1969.

Chapter 8: Coping With Stress and Change

1. Hans Selye, *Stress Without Distress*, Signet, 1974.

Chapter 9: Developing a Healthy Mental Attitude Toward Change

1. Rudyard Kipling, Poem: "If", 1895.
2. William P. Morgan, In: *The Marathon: Physiological, Medical, Epidemiological, and Psychological Studies*, Paul Milvy, Ed., New York Academy of Sciences, 1977.
3. Martin E. P. Seligman and Mihaly Csikszentmihalyi, "Positive Psychology: An Introduction," *American Psychologist*, 2000.
4. Marilyn L. Fox, Deborah J. Dwyer and Daniel C. Ganster, "Effects of Stressful Job Demands and Control on Physiological and Attitudinal Outcomes in a Hospital Setting," *The Academy of Management Journal*, 1993.
5. Kate Sparks, Brian Faragher and Cary L. Cooper, "Well-being and Occupational Health in the 21st Century Workplace," *Journal of Occupational and Organizational Psychology*, 2001.

6. Paul E. Spector, "Perceived Control by Employees: A Meta-Analysis of Studies Concerning Autonomy and Participation at Work," *Human Relations*, 2002.

Chapter 10: Communicating Change
1. William Shakespeare. *Henry V*, Act III, Scene I.
2. *Apollo 13* is a 1995 film portrayal, directed by Ron Howard, of the ill-fated Apollo 13 lunar mission. The movie was adapted by William Broyles, Jr. and Al Reinert from the book *Lost Moon* by Jim Lovell and Jeffrey Kluger.
3. Daniel Yankelovich, *The Magic of Dialogue—Transforming Conflict Into Cooperation*, Simon and Schuster, 1999.
4. The Belfast Agreement (also known as the Good Friday Agreement and, more rarely, as the Stormont Agreement) was a major political development in the Northern Ireland peace process. It was signed in Belfast on April 10th 1998 (Good Friday) by the British and Irish governments and endorsed by most Northern Ireland political parties. It was endorsed by the voters of Northern Ireland and the Republic of Ireland in separate referenda on May 23, 1998.

Chapter 11: Understanding Your Desire

Chapter 12: Understanding Your Ambition
1. Henri J. M. Nouwen, *Reaching Out*, Doubleday, 1986.
2. Martin Buber, *I and Thou*, Free Press, 1971.
3. Carolyn Y. Woo, Martin J Gillen Dean and Ray and Milann Siegfried Professor of Management, in the Mendoza College of Business at The University of Notre Dame, Letter to *The Wall Street Journal*, June 25, 2001.
4. Alan Lakein, *How to Get Control of Your Time and Your Life*, Signet, 1989.

Chapter 13: Guiding Your Vision
1. James W. Smither, Mamuel London, Raymond Flautt, Yvette Vargas and Ivy Kucine, "Can Working With an

Executive Coach Improve Multi-score Feedback Ratings Over Time? A Quasi Experimental Field Study," *Personnel Psychology*, 2003.

2. Elizabeth C. Thach, "The Impact of Executive Coaching and 360-Feedback on Leadership Effectiveness," *Leadership and Organization Development Journal*, 2002.

3. Mike Jay, "How to Leverage Executive Coaching," *Organization Development Journal*, 2003.

4. B. H. Spitzberg and W. R. Cupach, *Handbook of Interpersonal Competence Research*, Springer-Verlag, 1989.

5. Séamus Heaney, *Death of a Naturalist*. Faber and Faber, 1966. Reprinted with permission.

Epilogue

1. Andrew Lloyd Webber and Tim Rice, Stage play (1968) and movie (1999), *Joseph and the Amazing Technicolor Dreamcoat.*

2. Tal Ben-Shahar, *Happier*, McGraw-Hill, 2007.

Acknowledgements

In truth, the last thing I had planned was to write a book! However, my resistance was challenged a few years ago by a business prospect in Atlanta to whom I was presenting McLaughlin Young's services. At first, I felt that the human resources executive was not paying attention. But when I was finished, she inquired, "Have you ever written a book?" I took the question as a compliment but revealed some of my concerns about popular leadership books.

She offered that if I ever decided to do so, she would like to introduce me to an acquaintance who owned a company that summarized business books. Two years later, at the insistence of my staff, I contacted John Fayad. John is now my literary coach. His insights and careful guidance throughout this project have been invaluable.

Closer to home, my daughter, Moira LoCascio, has been a particularly constructive reviewer and counselor throughout this literary journey. Additionally, I appreciate the input of several of my colleagues, in particular, Ron Pelt and Jeff Shook, who intimately understand the mission of McLaughlin Young.

Also, I extend my appreciation to friends and clients who have served as impartial readers of various drafts of this manuscript:

Dr. Phoebe Bailey, Neil Cafferky, Finian Carney, Carolyn Coleman, Paul Delahunt, Jim Graham, Dr. Amanda Harrell, Lucy Henry, Gregory Lashutka, Dr. Peter Lodge, Orson Mason, Susan McConnell, Lance Mitchell, Fintan Muldoon, Chuck Sarka, Margaret Siczek, and especially my dear friend Dr. Jal Mistri.

Finally, to my wife Mary Pat, thank you for your patience, example, insights, and wise counsel during this project, as well as throughout our life together.

Printed in the United States
141172LV00001B/10/P